Norma Jean

Behavior Matters
Making Child Care Work for You

Deborah Hewitt
with Yvonne Pearson

D1712257

Redleaf Press
St. Paul, Minnesota
www.redleafpress.org

Published by Redleaf Press
a division of Resources for Child Caring
10 Yorkton Court
St. Paul, MN 55117
Visit us online at www.redleafpress.org.

© 2005 Redleaf Press
Cover design by Lightbourne
Cover illustration by Patrice Barton
Typeset in Adobe Caslon

Redleaf Press books are available at a special discount when pur-
chased in bulk for special premiums and sales promotions. For details,
contact the sales manager at 800-423-8309.

Library of Congress Cataloging-in-Publication Data
Hewitt, Debbie, 1958-
  Behavior matters : making child care work for you / Deborah
Hewitt with Yvonne Pearson.-- 1st ed.
     p. cm. -- (Redleaf guides for parents)
  Includes bibliographical references.
  ISBN-13: 978-1-929610-73-0
  ISBN-10: 1-929610-73-4
 1. Child care--United States. 2. Children of working parents--
United States. 3. Temperament in children. I. Pearson, Yvonne. II.
Title. III. Series.
  HQ778.63.H49 2005
  362.71'2'0973--dc22
                                    2005015435

Manufactured in the United States of America
12 11 10 09 08 07 06 05   1 2 3 4 5 6 7 8

Printed on acid-free paper.

Behavior Matters

Foreword

Making Child Care Work for You

You are among the more than half of working parents in the United States who have made the momentous decision to put their young children into child care. Whether you have chosen a private center, a school-based program, or a family child care provider, you want this to be a place where your child will be nurtured, safe, and provided with challenging, developmentally appropriate learning experiences.

Reading this book places you among those parents who want to take an ongoing active role in ensuring that their child has a quality child care experience. Advancing quality child care has been the mission of Redleaf Press and its parent nonprofit organization, Resources for Child Caring, for over thirty years. When women began entering the workforce in record numbers in the 1970s, Resources for Child Caring was one of the first organizations in the country to help parents find child care and advocate for quality child care for all children. We know children, child care, early education, and what parents value. As a leading publisher of educational materials for child care professionals, Redleaf Press has brought together its knowledge and resources—including authors who are nationally recognized experts in the field—to create the Redleaf Guides for Parents series.

This series offers practical, easy-to-implement suggestions for enriching your child's experience in child care. Early childhood experts have identified the quality of that experience as an important ingredient in preparing your child for school. Recent brain research has revealed how critical the first five years are to a child's development. During these years the brain grows at its fastest rate, and connections between neurons in the brain are made rapidly. It is these connections that are the underpinnings of language and cognitive development, emotional well-being, and social skills. The nurture and stimulation you provide at home to foster these connections should be extended and enhanced by what your child encounters every day in child care.

This Redleaf Guide covers critical issues that you will want to explore with your provider as you become partners in creating a stimulating and nurturing continuum of care and learning for your child. We at Redleaf Press wish you great success in building a collaborative relationship that is mutually enjoyable and productive for you, your provider, and most important, your child.

Eileen M Nelson

Eileen Nelson
Director, Redleaf Press

Introduction

Parents worry. It seems to go with the job description. They worry about whether their child is eating enough and growing well. They worry about whether their child is assertive enough, or too assertive. They worry about whether their child's behavior is the normal stuff of growing up or if it's out of bounds.

No matter how much delight you take in your children, you've probably been surprised by how difficult taking care of them is, especially when they hit that toddler stage. They want to do everything for themselves, whether or not the tasks are beyond their ability. They want to smear the peanut butter on the toast themselves, but if you let them, it gets all over the counter, their face, and probably your new shirt as well. If you don't let them, they throw a fit. Is this normal? Yes. Is it easy? Obviously not. Children's behavior can be both utterly normal and very challenging at the same time.

One of the biggest concerns working parents have is how their children are doing in child care. They wonder if they've chosen the best place for them, if they're happy there, and if they're getting all the attention and care they deserve. They want to know that the child care center or family child care provider is giving their children what they would get at home, that their children are getting excellent guidance and teaching and nurturing.

Child care can offer your child great advantages.

Child care centers and family child care settings can provide children with opportunities and resources to get ready for kindergarten, first grade, and beyond that aren't even available at home. They learn about interacting with other children and adults. They learn communication skills, how to get their needs met, how to be respectful of other people and themselves at the same time. They discover the joy of learning and they experience caring and nurturing relationships with adults other than their parents. So what is the parent's role in all this?

This book is one in a series that helps parents become active partners with their child care providers and teachers to ensure that their children do get the best care possible. How can you work with these persons who are regularly involved in teaching new skills during some of the most important stages of development in your child's life? How much can you ask from them? What if they do things differently than you do? What if they aren't doing some things you think your child needs and deserves?

About This Book

The focus of this book is how you can effectively establish an ongoing working relationship with your child care provider to address some of these questions as they relate to one of the most fundamental early childhood issues: your child's behavior. This book also addresses some basic developmental information that goes hand-in-hand with understanding behavior challenges. At the end of the book, you'll find suggestions for additional material you can read for more in-depth information about children's developmental needs and stages.

The following chapters discuss how you can partner with your provider in coping with behavioral challenges and teaching new behavior skills. Each chapter offers brief developmental information keyed to ideas for coping with the behavior and for partnering with your provider to shape new behaviors. The book is organized so that you can skip directly to the chapters that are relevant for you at any given time. For instance, if you are past the toilet training stage but are working with your child around sitting still long enough to eat, you can go directly to Chapter 5.

Since the profession is dominated by women, we refer to the provider as "she" throughout this book. We alternate between "he" and "she" when referring to children. Even though we talk mostly about child care in centers and homes, the ideas we present are relevant to preschool, Head Start, and early childhood family education settings as well.

Chapter 1
The Child Care Experience

Your child probably spends a significant portion of his time with a child care provider. It's important, then, that you be aware of a provider's basic childrearing philosophy as you look for child care. In this chapter we consider briefly some childrearing practices that have been proved to nurture self-esteem, confidence, good social skills, and a caring attitude. We'll then talk about some of the things to look for as you choose a child care setting and provider, and how to form a good partnership with your provider. If you're a new parent, you may find it useful to first read Chapter 17, where we review some of the latest information on child development and some principles of childrearing in a little more depth. Such information can help guide you as you decide how to deal with specific behaviors.

A Few Words on Childrearing Practices
Research suggests that the best way to help your child learn new behaviors is through what's called a guidance approach, which can be summed up by the phrases

"Guide rather than punish" and "Teaching works better than blaming." A guidance approach focuses on building nurturing relationships, preventing inappropriate behavior, finding ways to solve problems, and working with others to help your child. It is really an educational approach.

Let's look at an example. Jose is a two-and-a-half-year-old charmer, outgoing, busy, and full of curiosity. His parents laugh a lot when they tell stories about his exploits. But some of his exploits make them crazy at the same time. Jose has a ton of energy—and he's a climber. His father, who works part-time and is home with Jose in the afternoons, often finds him inside cupboards and on top of chairs and tables.

One day he left Jose in the kitchen for about three minutes while he ran down to the laundry. After running back upstairs, he couldn't see Jose. In a panic, he started running through the house calling for him. He finally found him standing on top of the refrigerator. That experience proved to him that three minutes was too long to leave Jose alone.

Notice that Jose's dad didn't focus on what Jose was doing wrong. He didn't tell himself that Jose was being bad or disobedient. Instead, he realized that Jose simply was a ball of energy and that ball had to find ways to bounce. He saw his job as providing ways for Jose to spend his abundant energy safely, and teaching him how to hear "no" when he needed to.

Most children are full of energy. They are by nature inquisitive adventurers. It's their job to explore and learn about life. And it's the job of adults to guide their explorations. It's important to remember that what children are doing, even when it feels difficult to adults, usually is a normal and natural part of their growth. It's normal for young children to feel mad and hit before they learn how to express anger appropriately. It's normal for them to feel frustrated and have temper tantrums on the way to learning coping skills. Challenging behavior is part of the normal growth of children as they go through different developmental stages. When you remember this, it's much easier to embrace the joy of channeling your children's energy and facilitating their growth.

Choosing a Provider and a Setting

Your child care provider spends critical hours with your child, perhaps every day. She has the job of teaching him behavioral skills right along with you. Your teaching will be more effective if you and your child care provider are giving your child the same messages. So it's important that you choose a child care provider who views and teaches children the way you want your child to be seen and taught.

If you are just choosing or just starting with a new provider, whether at a child care center, at a preschool, or in a family child care setting, don't be afraid to ask questions. Some behavior-related questions you might want to ask include the following:

- How might you handle a time when my child misses me and is crying?
- How might you handle it if my child becomes frustrated

with a puzzle and pushes it off the table?
- What kinds of food do you serve, and what are your rules around eating?
- What do you do when one child hits another?
- Do you have regular nap times, and what are your rules around napping?
- How would you handle it if my child wet her clothes?
- In general, what is your philosophy around discipline?

Depending on the type of setting you've chosen, there will be differences in how formal discipline and behavior philosophies are—for example, if there are written policies, if there is staff training and evaluation, and if practices are followed consistently. If you've chosen a center with multiple providers, there may even be differences among staff. You'll need to tailor your inquiries according to the setting; what's important is that you establish an ongoing dialogue on these issues and that you make your needs and expectations clear in the beginning and as incidents occur and questions arise.

The Parent/Provider Partnership

Whether you're just starting out with a new center or day care home or have had your child in a setting for some time, building and sustaining a trusting, open relationship with the provider and collaborating on the key elements of your child's care are priorities. What follows are some basic principles and practices that top child care professionals and experts agree are essential to establishing a successful collaborative relationship.

> Share Information

When your child first starts attending a new center or family child care home, you need to give your provider important information, such as what kinds of food your child likes to eat, whether or not she naps at home and how long, how she tends to relate to other children, and where she is in toilet training. And then you should continue to communicate as these issues change and as new things come up. Let your provider know if there are any new stresses in your child's life, if her sleep patterns are changing, if she's gotten especially clingy, and what you're doing at home to address these things.

By the same token, find out what's happening at child care. Ask questions about the activities they're doing, what they're eating, how much they're sleeping, what your child's relationships with other children are like.

When you're teaching certain behavioral skills at home, coordinate approaches with your child care provider. For instance, if you're trying to teach your child to ask for help when he gets frustrated, work with your provider to see if she can give your child the same kinds of suggestions. If you're trying to teach your child to take turns, find out how well she takes turns at child care and what the provider does to help with this. In the chapters following this one, you'll find specific ideas for coordinating with your child care provider on various ways of handling the key tasks your child must tackle in his early years.

It's also helpful to your provider if you let her know about any particular stresses—good or bad—that your child may be under. This might include relatives coming for a visit, the death of a relative or friend, a parent getting a new job, a change in routine, and so on. One common stress these days is divorce. If you are going through a separation or a divorce, be sure to inform your provider. Divorce is stressful for everyone involved, including the children, who undoubtedly will have different reactions at different stages of the process. For example, when they first find out, they may temporarily return to earlier stages of development, such as wetting their clothes or having more tantrums. If your provider knows what's happening at home, she can help give your child a steady environment and reassurance.

One caution in communicating on these more complex issues: don't try to cover everything at drop-off and pick-up times. It's very tempting to do this, because it's convenient. But it can also result in frustration for you, for the provider, and most of all, for your child. You son or daughter has been playing hard and is tired and eager to see you at the end of the day. Generally your child needs your full attention at this time. If you and the provider focus on each other instead, your child may act out even more in order to get your attention.

In addition, if you have a special concern you want to talk about with the provider, it may be something your child shouldn't overhear. For example, it's probably better if Yassi doesn't hear her dad say, "Yassi is so cranky these days. She's driving me crazy. Has she been especially cranky here too?" and then hear the provider say, "Yes, Yassi has been unusually grouchy. She knocked over Sarah's block tower today, and she threw a puzzle on the floor when I brought it to her."

To discuss these and other complex topics, you might make an appointment to meet, perhaps when the children are napping. Or you might designate a time to talk on the telephone. That way, your child will not be over-hearing conversations about her that she may experience as negative, and you and your child care provider will be free to talk honestly and openly without taking important time away from the children.

>Take Advantage of What Your Provider Can Teach You

Child care providers often have years of experience with many children, children of all different temperaments and activity levels and at different stages of development. Your provider may also witness things about your child that you don't get to see. The child care setting makes demands on your child that he probably never faces at home, such as demands to interact with more and different children and to function in a larger group setting. Because of this broad experience, your child care provider may have valuable insights into your child's behavior. She can probably tell you, too, a lot about what's typical of a child the same age as your child.

Still, it can be awfully hard to hear from a provider that she has a concern about your child, or that your child is behaving in a difficult way. Often a parent's first reaction is to think, "Not my child. There must be some-thing wrong with the provider." Another frequent reac-tion is to feel ashamed. "I must not be a very good parent. I can't get my child to behave as well as the other kids." While understandable, neither of these reactions is very helpful. No parent can always get his or her children to behave in a certain way. It might be something that the provider is doing wrong, but it might not.

It can be especially hard to hear from a provider that she thinks you need to get professional help for your child. If it has been strongly recommended and you are hesitant to do so, think about why. Is it because you really don't agree? Or is it that you don't know where to call, or don't have the money, or don't trust doctors or counselors? First be honest about why this is so hard for you to hear, and then decide what action to take. You might ask your provider for ideas about where to call or how to check into getting financial help. Before you rule it out, you might make an appointment with your provider so you'll have plenty of time to talk and get a better understanding of why she thinks your child needs counseling.

If you believe that the child care setting is a good one, then the provider may have useful information for you. Remember that she, too, has the best interests of your child at heart. Try to remain open to what she has to say and try to think of her feedback as an opportunity to learn valuable things about your child.

>Be Willing to Compromise
We've talked about trying to keep consistency between the child care setting and home—napping at the same time, teaching the same behaviors, responding to difficult behaviors in the same way, and so on. The child care provider may make requests of you, and you may have some special things you'd like the provider to do. There

are some times, however, when the provider simply cannot make special adaptations. Providers typically have more children to care for than you do at home. The time they can give to any one child is limited.

This may mean, for instance, that if your child needs a special diet, you'll have to fix it at home and take it to child care. You might want a written report on your child at the end of each day or each week. Your provider may not have time to do this, and you'll need to compromise. Perhaps you could arrange some telephone time each week for a report, or the provider could send home a sheet with stars or some other acknowledgement at the end of each day that indicates the progress your child is making on a certain behavior. Perhaps your child is ready to stop napping, but the child care provider needs those twenty minutes of quiet time each afternoon to do paperwork or planning. You might suggest that your child be allowed to look at books quietly or listen to music on headphones instead of trying to sleep. You would, however, probably have to supply any special materials, such as the tape recorder and headphones.

It's also possible that the provider will ask you to make some compromises. For instance, your child may have a favorite toy she'd like to bring to child care, but your provider has a no-toys-from-home policy, which is a common practice because children expect to be able to play with all the toys. The child care provider might ask that you make it an at-home-only toy or that you donate similar or duplicate toys for the other children to use.

Sometimes your provider may ask things of you that don't really make sense, or you may misinterpret what she's asking you to do. For instance, she may tell you about something frustrating your child did during the day, and you think she's expecting you to discipline your child. In a case like this, you should first confirm what her expectations are; she may just be sharing this information so you know what's going on rather than expecting any response. If it turns out she is expecting some action on your part, this may not make sense, because your child won't connect your response later at home to what he did earlier at child care. In such an instance, you could support the provider by talking about the incident with your child and then doing something more instructive than disciplinary by reading books that address the behavior or using a puppet to act out the situation and focusing on how to work it out the next time.

> Show Appreciation

It's helpful for you to periodically let your provider know you appreciate what she's doing for your child. You might bring her a small gift, or simply tell her what you like about the ways she helps your child learn and grow. If your child makes an enthusiastic report about something that happened at child care or something she learned, let the provider know. Providers often don't see the positive outcome of things they do, so this kind of feedback can mean a lot. Here are some ideas for inexpensive gifts that can let your provider know her work matters to you: a thank-you card, a picture your child made that's been put in a frame, a purse-sized bottle of lotion, homemade cookies that you and your child made together, a balloon, flowers, a stack of paper plates, a new toy for the center, or an offer to go to the library and check out books for her.

When You Can't Come to an Agreement with Your Child Care Provider

There are lots of reasons why parents and providers have disagreements. Some providers have strong opinions about how children should behave and how they should be disciplined when they don't. A provider may see a behavior during the day that parents don't see at home. A child may react differently in a group of children than she does at home with siblings or just one or two play-mates. A certain behavior may be just fine at home but difficult in a group setting. For example, a child may want to leave the table at lunch, go play, and then come back and eat some more. This might work at home, but in a child care center, with the demands of a more struc-tured schedule and many children to watch, it will make life very difficult.

The key to solving disagreements with anyone, including providers, is honest, open, and respectful com-munication. Just as it's hard for you to hear from your provider that your child is having a problem, it can be hard for a provider to hear that something isn't working well on her watch. Remember that most providers care about the children they take care of and want to do the best job possible. Be tactful when you raise a concern with your provider. Along with what you want changed, tell her about what she's doing well.

Don't let problems fester. If you don't talk about a problem until you're really frustrated, it will be much harder to be reasonable and objective. If you have different ideas about how to approach a problem, express them clearly and respectfully, but be flexible and respect the other person's thoughts and ideas also. Always focus on your child and what she needs instead of defending your opinions, and don't get caught up in a power struggle with your provider.

Some parents decide to move their child to a new child care setting when the going gets rough. This may be necessary, but be cautious about making this decision impulsively. Sometimes hanging in there and working things through can help you learn important things about and for your child, and your child won't have to adapt to a new situation unnecessarily. Changing settings can make your child feel that he's been a failure. Changing settings isn't likely to fix things if the problem lies with your inflexibility on important issues or with problems your child has that you're having difficulty facing.

Still, there are times when changing settings may be the best thing for you and your child. Here are some things to look for that might indicate the need for a change in child care.

- When you and the provider can't come to a compromise on something you really value.
- When you and the provider can't come to agreement generally or in specific key instances on how to deal with behavior challenges and how to teach new behaviors to your child.
- When your child protests and cries for weeks, even after

you and the child care provider have tried to address your child's needs in every way you can think of. Evaluate such a situation carefully, for it may indicate a larger problem that has nothing to do with the specific setting.

- When your child has been successfully attending the child care for a period and then begins protesting or crying for no apparent reason.
- If lack of compliance with standards or staff issues arise that cause you to question the quality of care your child is getting. Even if a setting is excellent when you enroll your child, staff changes, personal problems with the provider, and other factors can change the picture.

It's possible that a specific child care setting is simply not a good fit for your child. You can do all the research in the world, find a wonderful place, and it still might turn out not to be the right place. For instance, you may discover that your child's temperament causes him to feel overwhelmed by the commotion at a large center, and he is more comfortable in a smaller family child care setting. Or, though your daughter has been quite happy in her home care setting, several children her age have recently left and she no longer has playmates she relates to because most of the remaining children are quite a bit younger than she is.

It's also possible that the child care provider isn't a good fit for your child. The majority of child care providers are caring people who truly have your child's best interests at heart. But they're not perfect any more than parents are perfect. You may discover that the provider you've chosen is more punitive with your child than you like, or that a provider isn't as well trained or as flexible as you need. If your child has a particularly challenging behavior or is vulnerable in some way, he may need a more highly skilled provider than many other children do.

When all is said and done, you know what's best for your child. And when you do find a provider you like and trust, building a collaborative relationship based on trust, sharing, compromise, and mutual commitment to do what's best for your child will relieve most of your concerns about child care and make it a positive and fruitful experience for you and your family.

• • •

Points to Remember and Discuss

- It's important to share information about changes or stressors.
- Children need a parent's full attention at the end of the child care day.
- The parent and the provider can learn from each other.
- Both need to be flexible and make compromises.
- A relationship is built with open, honest communication.
- Parents need to show providers that they appreciate their work.
- Even very good child care settings are not a good fit for every child.

Chapter 2
Don't Go, Mommy:
Separating

What's Normal

Going to child care for the first time, or going to a new child care setting, is usually difficult for a child. In fact, being left by Mom or Dad in any place that's not familiar provokes separation anxiety. Separation anxiety generally becomes very intense for babies when they are around eight months old, and again at about the age of eighteen months.

Preschool-age children are usually past the worst of separation anxiety, but that doesn't mean it's gone. When they are in unfamiliar circumstances, children still find it frightening to be separated from the person who provides their sense of security. For that matter, children generally experience some separation anxiety even when they're going off to college or their first job, and we adults may experience it, for instance, when we leave those we love to go on a trip. Learning to cope with separation anxiety is an important skill we need throughout our lives.

How intensely any given child experiences separation anxiety varies greatly. It will depend on her previous experiences and her temperament. Your child may be one of those who is very extroverted, rushes into new places, and appears to have no anxiety at all. Or your child may cry and cling to you when it's time for you to leave. Sometimes children will withdraw and refuse to talk. Even the least anxious child will probably need some help in making the transition to child care.

Preparing for Going to Child Care

There are a number of things you can do to help your child with anxiety about separating from you when he starts child care, is going into a new setting, or is just reacting to something stressful in his life. First, in new settings, you can ask the provider if you can bring your child for a visit and be allowed a phase-in time. You can do a short visit the first time and lengthen your stay on subsequent visits. Play near your child at first, and then move to the side of the room and watch. You will still be present so your child can look over and see you, and then when she feels safe, she can go about her playing. Once she seems comfortable, you can say goodbye and take a short walk or read a book outside, increasing your time away until she is comfortable.

Often just one or two visits are enough for a child, or it might take several visits over one or two weeks. It really depends on your child's temperament. If you can't take several visits over the time away from work to help your child with a gradual transition, perhaps the child's other parent can take turns with you, or a grandparent or other trusted adult can substitute. In any event, some phase-in time will help your child let go of you more easily each day. Even if your child has been in child care before and is just moving to a new setting, a phase-in time can be very helpful.

There are also other ways you can help prepare your child. You can read with your child books about other children going to child care. Preschoolers can be encouraged to see this as an exciting chance to be a "big kid." You can present a positive image of the new setting by talking about the kinds of things your child will do there. You might even ask the provider if she'd be willing to check with another parent about introducing your children and letting them play together. That way your child would know another child the first time she is left there.

You can play "child care" with your child by pretending that you are in a child care center. Find out what words the provider uses for various activities and use them during your playtime. These might include words such as "group time," "snack time," and "free play." You can incorporate your leaving into your pretend time, and take turns being the one who is leaving and the one who is being left.

If it's not against a home or center's policy, talk with your provider about letting your child bring a special toy—perhaps a favorite doll or stuffed animal—or blanket with him in the beginning to ease the transition. Such "transitional objects," as child development experts call them, help your child take a little bit of home with him. You could also send a photo of you and your child that he could keep with him or tape to his cubby.

When It's Time to Say Goodbye

Saying goodbye is the hardest part. Lots of parents find it very painful to walk out the door when their child is clinging to them and begging them not to leave. What parents often don't realize is that children often begin playing happily with other children about fifteen seconds after the parent is no longer in sight. Ask your provider how long it takes your child to settle into the routine after you leave. This is important information that may be very comforting to you.

Sometimes it's tempting to just sneak out without saying goodbye. You tell yourself your child will avoid the pain of separating if you do this, and you know you'll avoid the pain of watching your child cry or beg for something you can't give him. Still, it's not a good idea. Sneaking out teaches your child to be wary about when you may leave and can actually increase future anxiety.

When you say goodbye, do it quickly. Accept your child's fear. Don't shame her. Don't say things like "Big girls don't cry." And don't try too hard to talk your child out of it. If you work overtime to protect her from her fear, she may end up believing there really is something to be scared of. Be honest about your own feelings, but make sure you don't let your anxiety rub off on your child. By now, you're probably thinking you have to walk the perfect line between too much reassurance and too little. But there is no perfect line. Just try to be matter-of-fact. You might say, "I'll miss you, too, but I know there are lots of fun things to do here. And I'll be back soon." Then leave.

Most providers understand how to help children make this transition. They'll give your child one-on-one attention if he's having trouble settling down when you leave. They'll involve him with an activity or with another child, comfort him, and give him reassurance.

You have the right to ask questions about how the provider helps your child with separation anxiety. Feel free to ask her how she handles your child's fear when you leave. But remember to be tactful. Most providers know their business well and care about the children they're watching. So approach the conversation with respect and in a spirit of information sharing. Instead of saying, "I want to make sure you're doing this right. My child needs your full attention when I walk out the door," you might say, "Leaving my child is hard for me. I'll feel better if I know what's happening after I leave. Can you tell me what you do with him after I walk out the door?"

You can also make suggestions. You know your child better than anyone else does. Your provider will probably appreciate information about things such as a special book your child loves or a song that she finds comforting. In such a case, you might want to provide the book or the music.

When Separation Anxiety Develops Later
Sometimes a child who has appeared to be well adjusted to a child care setting suddenly starts to become tearful or upset when you drop her off. This could be a delayed

reaction to separation, and you will once again need to spend the extra time and attention parents typically spend at the beginning of a new program or place. You can also watch to see if there is a pattern. Maybe Mondays are hard because your child hasn't been to child care during the weekend. Or there might be another source of anxiety. Has there been a change at home or in the child care setting? Has there been an upset with another child or adult? Is your child upset because she was disciplined for something? Is there an issue over naptime? Has a special friend or staff member left the program?

Whatever the cause, give the separation time special attention again. Create a routine around leaving home. Spend some extra cuddle time with your child before you take her to child care. Plan what you will do together when you get home. Brainstorm with your provider about whether there have been any changes at child care that could be creating anxiety for her. If naptime is difficult, maybe the provider can repeat as much of your home naptime routine as possible. Or perhaps she can make some mealtime or snacktime food that your child especially loves. Your child will get through this phase; the important thing is that you and the provider work together to support her.

Pick-Up Time

Ironically, sometimes a child who can barely stand to let a parent leave in the morning is having so much fun in the afternoon that he can barely stand to leave child care. Maybe he keeps running back to the toys or a friend he was playing with and refuses to leave. He may even start to cry or have a tantrum. You can tell him that you know it's hard to leave when he's having so much fun, and reassure him that he'll get to come back again and the toys and his friends will still be here. You can also tell him about something he can look forward to at home. If your child keeps resisting, you may need to say something like "Do you want to come now or in two minutes?" or, "You can come by yourself or I will carry you."

Ask the provider to give your child some warning as pick-up time approaches. Ask her to tell him that you are coming soon and he needs to get ready to go. If you're going to be unusually early or late, call ahead so your provider can prepare your child. Then be ready to spend a few minutes allowing your child to make the transition comfortably. And focus on him rather than talking with the provider.

There can be an awkward confusion between provider and parent at pick-up time. A parent who thinks the provider is still in charge may hang back, waiting for the provider to do something. At the same time, the provider who thinks the parent is in charge once he or she arrives will wonder why the parent isn't taking charge. Avoid any confusion by asking your provider which of you is to guide your child's behavior at pick-up time.

When Separation Anxiety Doesn't Go Away

When a child is very shy or very upset, separation issues may not go away. If you are having that experience, make sure the setting is a good match for your child. If your child is in a center, it's possible that the many activities and numerous children present are overwhelming for your child. The smaller setting of a family child care could be a better fit. The other children in a child care setting may be too different in age from your child. There may be too many babies and toddlers or too many older preschoolers, and your child has no one to play with. Even though you have chosen a high-quality child care setting, there may be things about it that make it a bad fit for your child.

If your child attends a child care center or family child care for three or four months and still cries for long periods every time she is dropped off, you may need to talk with a parent educator or counselor. Prolonged separation anxiety is difficult for everybody. Getting some extra help will benefit both you and your child.

• • •

Points to Remember and Discuss

- Although separation anxiety peaks at about eight months and again around eighteen months, even older preschoolers feel anxious about separating from their parents or other significant adults.
- Your child's temperament affects the amount of separation anxiety she experiences.
- You should arrange a phase-in period, visiting a new child care setting with your child at least one time and perhaps more.

- You need to be prompt, matter-of-fact, and reassuring when you say goodbye.
- You need to be clear about whether the provider or the parent is in charge at pick-up time.
- You need to consider whether prolonged protests mean that a particular child care setting is not a good fit for your child.

Chapter 3
No More Diapers:
Toilet Training

What's Normal

Most parents look forward to the day when their toddler is toilet trained. It's not that they necessarily resent having to diaper their child; diapers come with the territory. Still, there's freedom in not lugging a diaper bag everywhere you go, and, if you use cloth diapers, in not being met by that very particular scent when you pull the lid off the diaper pail. An end to diapering also cuts some costs. You know you don't want to push your child out of diapers before you should, but you sure want to move him along as soon as he's ready.

That's the puzzle, of course—recognizing when he's ready. You might be getting pressure from other parents. Maybe your neighbor or your friend has told you how she toilet trained her child when he was two years old. Maybe you're even getting pressure from your child care provider to get on with it. Despite such pressure, it's important to observe your own child and move ahead with toilet training only when he's ready.

The average age a child is toilet trained falls between two-and-a-half and three years for daytime dryness and between three and four years for nighttime dryness. And it's not unusual for some children to be trained even later than this.

When Do You Start?

How will you know when your child is ready? Sometime after your child's second birthday, watch for the following signs:

- Wants to imitate and please parent(s).
- Understands and follows simple directions, like "Pull down your pants" or "Sit on the stool."
- Stays dry for longer and longer periods.
- Seems aware of urination and bowel movements.
- Prefers to be clean and dry.
- Tries to pull pants up and down.

Your child care provider can be a great resource here. If she's worked with a lot of children, she probably recognizes the signs of readiness. Ask her if she has observed any of these signs in your child. Together you can decide if your child is ready to get started on this big step.

There are a couple of things to watch out for here. Either you or the provider might be eager to get going on toilet training simply because you're sick of changing diapers. Be careful not to start toilet training before your child also is ready. Doing so might lead to your child becoming anxious about this developmental milestone.

On the other hand, you might discover that although the child care provider is encouraging you to start toilet training, you are resisting. Try to determine whether this is because you really believe your child isn't ready, or because you think it might be easier to change diapers than to tackle the extra work of toilet training. If you think the latter might be true, then give training a try for just a couple of weeks and see what happens.

The other part of the puzzle is knowing the best ways to help your child master this complex task. Your child won't be completely toilet trained until he can notice the urge to use the toilet, get there in time, pull down his pants, use the toilet, pull up his pants, and wash up after himself. It's a big, complicated job, and it takes time.

Where Do You Start?

Let your child get used to the toilet. If he follows you into the bathroom, let him watch you use the toilet. If your child is in a child care center or a family child care, he may be watching other children about the same age use the toilet. You might check with your provider to see if this is the case. If not, you might ask your child care provider if it's okay for your child to begin watching others his age.

Let your child flush the toilet if he wants, or practice sitting on the stool. Start talking to him about these normal bodily functions. And ask your provider what terms for urinating and defecating are used at child care. It'll be less confusing for your child if you both use the same terminology. "Peeing" and "pooping" are terms that many people use.

Talk to your child as you change his diaper. You might say, "You pooped. Let's get you cleaned up. It feels good to be all clean." Avoid shaming words like "dirty" or "icky." Commenting on what's happening with your child's body helps him learn about these sensations. He first recognizes that he's wet or soiled. Then he recognizes when he's urinating. Finally, he learns to recognize what it feels like when he's about to wet.

Making a Concerted Effort

When your child seems ready to start using the toilet, you will need to make a concentrated effort for at least three to four weeks. Choose a time period when there are no major distractions, such as a new baby in the house or grandparents on a long visit. It's also very important to coordinate your effort with your child care provider. What you do at home will be more effective if you and the child care provider are doing similar things.

First, dress your child in pants that are easy to pull up and down. You may want to put him in toilet-training diapers such as Pull-Ups. Experts disagree about using these. Some people argue that a child needs to feel wet in order to prefer using the toilet. Others say Pull-Ups can help make a smooth transition from diapers to toilet.

If your child care provider has a preference different from yours, you'll need to figure out a compromise. For instance, you might think your child will learn more quickly if he feels the wetness in his pants. Your provider, especially if it's a center, may have so many children to tend to that dealing with repeated accidents is very difficult. Center staff may not want your child taken out of diapers until he's pretty reliably toilet trained. Wearing Pull-Ups at child care may be a compromise in this case. If you use a family provider, she may not mind moving directly from diapers to pants but probably will want to use Pull-Ups on field trips.

The next step is to take your child to the bathroom periodically throughout the day, after waking, after each meal, before going outside, and so on. Stay with him, singing songs or reading books, so that he'll consider going to the bathroom a positive time. If there are no results within five minutes, praise the effort and say something like "Maybe the pee will come out next time." If you're using Pull-Ups and have had several successes, switch to training pants and help your child remember to use the bathroom.

It's normal for children to have accidents when they're first learning to use the toilet. When this happens, be matter-of-fact. You might say something like "Accidents happen. Next time we'll have to stop playing earlier to get to the bathroom on time." Your provider will appreciate your sending extra clothes to child care during this time so she has something to change your child into if he has an accident.

Your child may not be as ready as you thought. You may put him in training pants and the accidents are constant. You may have tried for ten days and your child made no real progress. Sometimes people feel that they or their child was a failure when this happens. It's important to remember that having such an experience doesn't mean there's anything wrong with you or your child. It may simply signal that your child needs a little more time to develop the necessary muscle control. Let a few months pass before trying again.

When Your Child Resists

Toddlers and early-preschool children are famous for saying "no." They are at a stage of development where they try to prove they are autonomous. They want to know that they are their own person. This attitude can get in the way of toilet training. Mom or Dad is not going to tell them what to do. And with this particular skill, you really can't tell them what to do. They are in charge of their bodies, and they will demonstrate this fact again and again. If you have this experience, it could mean that your child is not emotionally ready for toilet training, and you need to put it off. Or it could mean that you just need to alter your approach a bit. Try saying, "Let's go to the bathroom" rather than asking, "Do you have to go to the bathroom?"

A child might be frightened by the flushing noise, or by the possibility of falling in, or of monsters in the toilet. You can handle these fears by waiting until your child leaves the bathroom before you flush, or by using a small potty chair, toilet seat adapter, or step stool. You might need to command any monsters to get out of the toilet and tell them never to return.

If you thought your child was ready for toilet training but you find he is resisting, check in with your child care provider. See if her experience is similar and what methods she is using to deal with it. If instead your child is doing better at home than at child care, you need to explore with your provider what's working in one place and not in the other. If your child is scared of the big toilet at child care or is used to a certain type of potty chair or toilet seat adapter, it might help him feel comfortable if you provide the same equipment for day care.

Incentives

People often hold strong and contradictory opinions about whether incentives for using the toilet are a good idea, and you and your child care provider may disagree about it. You may want to use some trinkets such as stickers, a star on the calendar, pennies in a piggy bank, barrettes and bracelets, or small cars. If your child care provider is willing to use such incentives when your child is in her care, she probably would like you to supply them.

On the other hand, your provider may feel that she can't do this because it will raise expectations from the other children that she cannot meet, or that their parents do not want her to meet. If this is the case, perhaps the provider could give your child a star when he's successful, and you can give him his reward when you arrive home. Or you might just let his experiences be different at child care and at home. The learning should still transfer between settings. If you decide to use incentives, be clear that once the supply is gone, he won't need any more because he'll know how to use the toilet by then. When this happens, involve your child in another activity as soon as he's done using the toilet so he won't notice the lack of a trinket as much.

Nighttime Wetting

Nighttime dryness lags behind daytime dryness by months for many children and by years for some. Nighttime wetting is not usually considered a problem until a child is six or seven years old. You can help your child stay dry at night by dressing him in pajamas that are easy to take off, by lighting the way to the bathroom, and by helping him if he calls you.

Experts disagree about restricting fluid intake in the evening. Some say this tends to focus the child on wanting a drink. Some people also believe you should not wake a child to take him to the bathroom during the night because he doesn't learn to respond to his body's signals. Others disagree. In any case, you can make life easier for yourself by making up your child's bed with two sets of sheets and waterproof pads to make nighttime accidents easier to clean up. You can then strip one set and the bed will be ready to sleep in.

When to Get Help

Take your child for a medical exam if he experiences pain or burning during urination, has a weak or small stream of urine, always has damp underwear, or has persistent symptoms of diarrhea or constipation.

• • •

Points to Remember and Discuss

- The average age a child is toilet trained falls between two-and-a-half and three years for daytime dryness and between three and four years for nighttime. Some children are trained even later than this.

- Toilet training should start when your child is ready, not when you or your provider is ready.

- To start toilet training your child, let him watch and practice tasks like flushing the toilet or sitting on the toilet.

- Toilet training requires several weeks, and it's helpful if the provider and parent work on it simultaneously.

- If you find your child is not ready after all, stop and wait for a few weeks or months.

- Nighttime wetting is not usually considered a problem until a child is six or seven years old.

Chapter 4
I'm Not Eating That:
Finicky Eating

What's Normal

Children can be picky eaters. Preschoolers are busy exploring the world; part of that exploration is figuring out what they like to eat—and what they don't like to eat. There's a good reason why things often taste different to children than they do to adults. Children have more taste buds in a more concentrated area, so many foods are too strong for them. What tastes like a nicely spiced chili in your mouth might taste like an explosion to a child.

Children also have different temperaments and different sensory thresholds. Variations in texture or temperature may feel more intense to one child than to another. Children who are very sensitive to textural and other sensory changes may be slower to accept new foods. It's important to trust your child's preferences. If she really hates broccoli, let her choose a different way to get the nutrients broccoli provides.

Finicky eating is often more of a problem for the parent than for the child. It makes sense that you'll be disappointed when you've worked hard to cook a good meal and your four-year-old turns up her nose at it. But finicky eating is really only a problem if your child's nutritional needs are not being met.

Parents often get nervous that their children aren't eating enough or aren't getting a balanced diet. Watch over a period of a couple of weeks and see if this is true. Children may eat a lot one day and little the next, or they may eat ravenously for a month and then lose most of their appetite. Some children prefer one food for two or three weeks and then say it's "yucky" the next time you offer it. Many children store up calories before a growth spurt, growing out before they grow up. Healthy children can have very different calorie intake needs. Given nutritious choices and left to their own devices, children generally can be counted on to eat as much as they need. Let your child decide how much to eat.

Child Care Food Policies

If you haven't already enrolled your child in child care, check on the food program or policies when you're looking. A center might have a written policy and a group of menus you can look at. A formal policy might include statements such as these:

- Good, nutritious foods will be offered.
- The child will be encouraged to try new foods.
- Manners and appropriate mealtime behaviors will be taught.

A family child care is apt to be less formal, but the provider should still be able to tell you her views regarding menus and mealtimes.

Providers do their best to offer nutritious foods that children like. Many of them work with food programs that help to monitor their menu planning and provide them with consultation about recipes and meals that appeal to young children. While providers work hard to promote healthy eating, they also have limited flexibility to tailor each meal for each child. Cooperative planning can be essential in meeting your child's unique needs. If you have concerns about a lack of nutrition or too much sugar in the meals your provider serves, talk to her about it tactfully. If she is unable or unwilling to make adjustments to her menu and this is a big concern for you, you will have to decide if you want to prepare meals for your child to take to day care. Depending on how serious the problem is and how important this factor is to you, you may decide to find another setting that provides the kind of nutritious foods you require.

Providers sometimes want children to eat independently earlier than they do in their home setting. Children are fed by their parents longer in some cultures than in others. You may be surprised when your provider asks you to encourage your child to feed herself, especially if your provider is of a culture different from yours. If you are asked this, it doesn't mean the provider thinks you have been doing it wrong. It is simply difficult for a provider to feed the young children herself when she is caring for many at the same time.

Let's look at some basic ideas for supporting a child in developing good eating habits and appropriate mealtime behaviors. These are things that you and your child care provider can do as partners.

No Force Feeding

While you don't want to be a short-order cook and make what each family member requests for each meal, keep your child's preferences in mind when you're planning family menus. If you love salmon and your child can't abide it, make sure there's some macaroni and cheese on the menu as well. If she'd rather have a peanut butter sandwich at times, that's fine. It's easy to fix, and nutritious. Accept her preferences and don't force her to eat things she doesn't like. Let her pass up the portabello mushrooms if she hates them.

It might help if you imagine you're traveling in another country and are presented with a dish you've never seen before. It looks unappetizing to you. You taste it and find it has a strong flavor that you really dislike, but you feel pressure to eat all of it just the same. Perhaps you almost gag when you swallow, but you know your host will be offended if you don't eat it. Would forcing it down help you to expand your appreciation of a new food? Probably not. This may be how your child feels when she's forced to eat a food she hates.

Let your provider know what foods your child hates and what she loves. This is especially useful when your child is entering a new place. Then the provider can be aware of her preferences as she plans her menus. If your child is having trouble with the food at day care, perhaps there is a typical meal your provider fixes that contains nothing your child really likes. Again, let your provider know. But remember to be tactful. You might says something like "Ellen likes so much of the food you make at your house. But there are a couple of meals you serve regularly that she just doesn't like. If you let me see your weekly menu plan in advance, I'll send a lunch from home on the days you serve those meals."

If your family culture is different from your provider's, your child may be used to eating things that are never on her menu. Talk to your provider about her policy and see if you could bring a special dish to your child's center or family child care. You may well enrich the food habits of your provider and the children and make your child feel special at the same time. Be aware, however, that regulations may require some child care settings to serve only food that has been prepared in inspected kitchens. If this is the case, you may have to buy that special dish rather than make it yourself.

Special Diets

If your child requires a special diet all the time, you may have to provide her meals yourself. Child care centers often have their meals provided by a central kitchen that cannot accommodate special diet requests. Even a family child care provider may not have the time to cook a different meal for one child every day.

If you find yourself in the position of providing a different meal for your child, you might want to check with the provider to see what she's planning to serve so your child's meal will not be vastly different. For instance, if the provider is serving cooked vegetables, you might want to send steamed rather than raw carrots. Children generally don't like to be very different from their peers. If your child requires a special diet, you might look for a child care setting where all the children bring their own lunches.

Adding New Foods

When you're trying to encourage your child to try something new, serve the new food as just an extra added to the meal. Then ask her to try one taste. Talk with your provider to see if you and she can adopt consistent approaches. And remember that new foods need to be introduced as many as ten times before a child considers them familiar and is likely to eat them. You can also try preparing foods in different ways. Vegetables can be eaten with dip, steamed, in soup, in a casserole, or with sauce or cheese. Brightly colored foods are eye-catching and more appealing. If your child tells you enthusiastically about a new food she's eaten at child care, ask your provider for the recipe so you can make it at home. You can also ask your provider to let you know whenever your child tries a new food and likes it.

A Matter of Hunger

Your child may resist eating simply because she's not hungry. A child's stomach is about the same size as her fist, so she requires smaller amounts of food than you do but needs to eat more often throughout the day. Children need snacks between meals; be sure the snacks you offer are nutritious.

Watch to be sure your child doesn't fill up on water, milk, or juice just before a meal or at the beginning of a meal. Try offering half a serving of her beverage along with the meal and the other half at the end. Make sure your child gets enough physical activity between meals to feel hungry again. You'll also want to ask your provider how much your child is eating while she's at child care.

Or a Matter of Time

Distractions can also interfere with hunger. Cartoons on television or a fascinating block tower might be so interesting that your child can't pay attention to a grilled cheese sandwich. One way to deal with this is to have regular mealtimes, perhaps timed similarly to mealtimes at child care, and to then alert your child when mealtime is approaching. Like the notice that you'll soon be picking her up at child care, this notice helps her get ready for what's coming next and eases the transition from playtime.

It can also help if you guide your preschooler to a calming activity before mealtime. Perhaps she can look at books or draw or do an activity in which she is basically sitting in one place. This can help her relax before mealtime and be prepared to sit for a while.

Sometimes children are slowpokes at the table. They may want to eat a bit, run off and play, and then come back again. You can begin altering such a pattern by setting a certain amount of time that your child must stay at the table and converse with other family members. After perhaps fifteen minutes, your child may need to move but still isn't done with her meal. You can allow her some time to move, but rather than keeping food on the table endlessly, set a certain amount of time for completing a meal, say thirty minutes. If your child is running back and forth, or playing with her food, gently remind her to concentrate. Let her know when there are only five minutes remaining before the meal is finished, and then firmly remove her food when that time comes. Your provider may have strict rules about remaining at the table. If she does, try to incorporate those rules at home to provide consistency and support.

Manners

Meals provide a good opportunity to teach good manners. You can ask your child to pass food and to say "please" and "thank you" when asking for and receiving food. Be sure, of course, that you model these manners as well.

Set limits about begging for things. Say, "We'll be eating what is offered; I know there are things you like and can fill up on, but this is what we're eating right now." Teach your child that there are respectful ways to decline food that she doesn't want to eat. Teach her to say, "No, thank you" rather than "I hate that."

Your provider is likely to be working on these same skills at the same time you are. Talk with her so you know exactly when and how she is working on them. Find out what manners she requires at mealtime. Your teaching will be reinforced if you both have similar rules.

Avoiding Power Struggles

When it comes to eating, parents can easily get stuck in the muck of power struggles. Children often decide to express their independence by declaring that they will not eat a certain food. Of course, this isn't a conscious decision. A child does not say to herself, "Today I'm going to show my mom that I'm in charge of my own life. How should I do this? I know. I'll refuse to eat lunch." Still, a child can get stuck in arguing about a food in order to pursue her valuable goal of asserting her independence.

As the adult, you can generally sidestep a fruitless tug-of-war. For instance, to offer healthy choices, you can say, "Would you like Cheerios or Rice Krispies for breakfast?" You can forgo rules such as finishing everything on the plate. You can decide to control what your child is offered, but let your child control how much she eats. You can avoid using sweets as a reward so that your child doesn't get accustomed to thinking dessert is more desirable than other foods.

Learning about Food

Children often like to play with the food on their plates. While this might mean they're not hungry anymore, it also might mean they're practicing their budding scientific skills. They may be curious about the food, about how the color looks when they mix the peas with the mashed potatoes, or about what shapes they can make out of food. Figuring out what foods are and how to feed yourself is a messy job. Children naturally make messes as they learn about food and meals.

Young children also may be messy in their eating because they're still working on eye/hand coordination. Many young children are still working on using forks and knives and spoons. And, depending on your culture, it's possible that your child is learning to use different utensils in your home. It takes time to learn to use a fork and knife and spoon or any utensil. Your provider is likely to be teaching these skills at mealtime. If this is an issue at home, confer with her about what she's doing and what she expects.

You can promote an interest in eating various foods by asking your child to help you pick out vegetables or snacks at the supermarket, or to help you prepare snacks. Preschool children can wash and scrub vegetables, tear lettuce, peel fruits, and open, pour, and stir mixes. They tend to love these active, hands-on ways of being involved with both you and food. According to their ability, children can also help with cleanup. Your child may also be able to help with food preparation and cleanup at child care, especially if she is in a family child care. If you notice particular tasks that interest your child, let your provider know.

• • •

Points to Remember and Discuss

• Children have more taste buds in a more concentrated area, so many foods are too strong for them.

- Children who are very sensitive to textural and other sensory changes may be slower to accept new foods.
- Providers may expect children to feed themselves earlier than parents do.
- You should include something your child likes at every meal, and you should let your provider know what foods your child loves or hates.
- Special diets or having your child bring food from home should be discussed with your provider.
- A new food should be just an extra to the meal. New foods need to be introduced as many as ten times before a child considers them familiar and is likely to eat them.
- Sometimes children resist eating because they are not hungry or because they are distracted.
- By offering choices to a child, you can sidestep power struggles.

Chapter 5
Let's Go, Go, Go:
Activity Level

What's Normal

As adults, we're apt to watch the exuberant energy of children and think, "Oh, to be able to go like that again!" Sometimes their energy level is challenging. Most parents breathe a sigh of relief when their children can finally sit still at the dinner table or wait comfortably in a line. But young children need to be able to move. Their bodies, and their brains, require a lot of activity.

Generally, young children have trouble sitting still or paying focused attention to anything for protracted periods. Children are increasingly active until they are three or four years old, when their activity level usually peaks. Most two-year-olds can usually sit and pay attention for only two or three minutes. Most five-year-olds can often pay attention for ten or fifteen minutes.

Some children are especially active. It seems like they just never stop. Sally is a good example. Although she's four years old, she can't be still for more than about five minutes. She is a challenge for her grandmother, who has custody of her. Although her grandma is crazy about Sally, she wears her grandma out. At mealtime, she spends more time out of her chair and running around the table than she does eating. When her grandma tries to read her a book, she fidgets and wiggles and runs off before the book is finished. Sally's grandma feels like she spends all day trying to keep up with her.

Although children like Sally are fun and stimulating, they can benefit from learning the skills of quieting themselves and paying attention. To function well in school and in groups, Sally must acquire these skills. But youngsters like Sally often get negative messages from adults who see them as willful or not willing to listen. This makes it especially important to protect their self-esteem while helping them learn to focus their energy.

High-Activity Levels in Child Care

Children with unusually high activity levels are generally more noticeable in child care settings than they are at home. It's usually easier to give one-on-one attention to and accommodate the unique needs of each child at home. In child care, where young children spend part of the day involved in group activities and usually are required to sit still in groups to listen to stories, a high-energy child will be more quickly noticed because he will tend to disrupt group times.

As a result, the parent of such a child is often surprised when a child care provider says, "Your son has so much energy. His activity level is so high that it makes it hard for him to learn. It also makes it hard for him not to disrupt story time. I think we need to help him learn to focus his energy more."

"Really?" the surprised parent may say. "I thought he was just like all the other kids."

And he may be "just like all the other kids," mostly. Being told your son or daughter has a high activity level is not a criticism and is not necessarily an indication of a behavioral or medical problem. Being highly active is often just another way of being in the world, and it simply means that he or she needs to learn another skill in order to do well in various settings.

Time, Toys, and Space for Moving

While all children need to move a lot, a high-activity child needs to move even more. If you are the parent of such a child, let him release energy by getting outside at least once every day if you possibly can. A child care center may have a playground where, weather permitting, he can run off energy each day. You, and the family child care provider, may have to be more inventive, but there are many ways to let him release energy. You, and perhaps your provider, can take him swimming, skating, for a hike, on a picnic in the park, or to the zoo.

You also can find ways for your child to burn off energy indoors. If he is in a child care center, he probably has climbing equipment and areas for what is called large motor activity—places to jump and roll and tumble and run. Although a family child care setting may not have formal play areas and learning environments, your child still can be given lots of opportunities for indoor movement in family child care and at home.

It's usually possible to have toys such as a minitrampoline or active "spin" and "twister" games. You can also have foam balls to throw into a basket, or let your child jump across a tape mark on the floor, drop pegs into a plastic jar, carry cotton balls on a spoon, or dance to music. One family child care provider put a covered mattress and box spring on the floor of a porch and called it the jumping room. Here, she let kids play actively under close supervision. To get ideas for home, ask your provider about large motor activities she does with the children. You can offer her suggestions from your experience as well.

There are also some activities that promote calming. Sensory activities—things like pouring sand from one container to another, making playdough shapes, playing with water, running fingers through cornmeal—can soothe an active child.

Helping Your Child Focus

The arrangement of space and toys can affect how well your child can focus. Too many toys or toys that are all in a jumble will make him feel more jumbled inside and less able to focus. Even decorations can do this. There has been a lot of emphasis on making a baby's room stimulating, with bright colors and pictures of faces on the walls and near the crib. This continues into preschool years, and people often paint their children's rooms bright colors or have colorful posters and pictures on the walls. Stimulation is great for young children, but there can be too much of a good thing. Too much stimulation can prompt a child to move from toy to toy, never really playing with anything. If your child has trouble focusing, you may want to tone down his environment visually, make it calm and orderly. This doesn't mean it has to be sterile. No one needs to be surrounded by blank white walls. But a calm environment can make it easier to focus.

If your child is easily stimulated, talk with your provider about measures you have discovered that help your child remain calm. You might say, "I've found at home that if I dim the lights, keep the toys organized, and don't have too many things on the wall, my child has an easier time settling down for naps." Providers aren't going to remove half the things from their walls, but many providers will be open to hearing what you have to say. Providers with training in child development will probably be quick to recognize your child's need for a calming environment. Family child care providers may have difficulty simplifying the environment a great deal since it is also their living space. Be aware, too, that if your child is easily stimulated, a child care setting that is highly stimulating may not be a good fit. If proper adjustments can't be made, you may want to find another setting.

If your child tends to wander from activity to activity and toy to toy, you can help him get started in the right direction. Ask him to choose what he wants to do when it's time to play alone. Then stay with him while he gets started. If he begins to wander without purpose, go to him and ask him what he wants to do next. Comment when he is engaged in an activity. Sally's grandmother learned to make comments such as "Sally, I love how you're working on building that road for your trucks. You are doing a great job."

At child care, one place where difficulty in focusing really shows up is during story time. You might also notice this at home when you are reading to your child. At child care, a high-energy child might start making noises while the book is being read, or get up and walk around, or squirm and bump into the child next to him, or poke his neighbor. Even one-on-one at home, your child might get restless before you can get through a picture book.

One way your provider might deal with this is by using attention grabbers at reading time, maybe starting with songs, or finger plays, or telling a flannelboard story. You can do this at home too. Read books that allow your child to touch, or pat, or open flaps. Tell stories with puppets, or act out stories. Ask questions as you read, or engage your child in trying to predict the end of the story. You can also keep story times short and read in a place that doesn't have a lot of distractions. Turn the television off. Tell your child when he's being a good listener.

You might also teach him about personal space. If he's having trouble at child care with nudging other children during story time, your provider can teach him about personal space, and you can teach him at home. Find out how your provider is teaching your child about personal space, and use some of the same techniques. You might also offer ideas to the provider. You can talk about personal space as a bubble. Ask your child to imagine a bubble around him that belongs only to him. Have him practice keeping his feet and hands inside that space while you read a story. You can't replicate the other children at child care sitting next to him in his bubble, but you can practice with stuffed animals. Ask your child to stay in the imaginary bubble and keep from knocking over the stuffed animals. This skill can then be transferred to child care.

Planning Outings and Other Changes

All children feel safer when their days are predictable, but children who have high activity levels seem to have an even greater need for this. They do best with predictable schedules and routines. They also need warnings when it's time to change activities. If your child is like this, give your provider a heads-up. Let her know you give him lots of warnings before transitions so she can be alert to his need. Give your child a warning well before it's time to leave for an outing. Then give him very clear instructions about what he needs to do. "Find your coat. Find your boots. Wait for me at the back door." If you're going to a place where you'll have to wait, maybe a doctor's office or a restaurant, bring along things that will help to occupy him. You might even ask him to pick out some small toys to bring along, perhaps tiny cars or crayons and a coloring book. Find out what outings your provider has planned so you can tell your child what to expect at child care the next day.

Impulse Control

We arrive in this world with almost no impulse control, and spend much of our childhood learning this important skill. Most of us still have trouble with it at times, even as adults. That new dress may have pushed you over your budget, but you fell in love with it. You probably would have had a better day at work if you hadn't stayed up so late watching that movie last night, but you thought, "What the heck." Or you didn't think.

Learning to control our impulses begins in childhood. We all have to learn that we can't just reach out and grab the food off someone else's plate because it looks good. We all have to learn that we can't shove somebody out of our path so we can go faster. High-activity children often have a difficult time learning to control their impulses. If you're wondering whether your child has an unusually hard time controlling his impulses, ask your provider for feedback. She'll be able to tell you how she sees him compared to other children his age.

Stop-and-freeze games can help children learn to control their impulses. Ask your child to jump or stop when you ring a bell. She should keep moving until you say her name, and then stop and freeze. This game can be a lot of fun for children and can also teach them to pay attention. You can play it at home with only your child or with your child and her playmates. You might also suggest the game to your provider. Although many providers have heard of this game and play it with children, your particular provider may not have.

Other ways to help children control their impulses

include getting down to their level and establishing good eye contact when you talk to them and, when you're asking them to stop a behavior, giving them alternatives. If your child is emptying the cupboards of all the pots and pans, you can get his attention and repeat the rule about not taking the pots out of the cupboards. Then give him an alternative, for example, "You can play with your toy dishes now." Or, "Why don't you go to your room and find your drum."

Sometimes impulsive behavior impinges on other children and leads to conflict. Sally frequently bumped other children in her hurry to get to the slide or the monkey bars at the playground. Her grandma started calling her name, going over to her, and helping her to notice the response of the other child. "Look at Tyrone's face. He looks really sad." Then she would ask Sally how she might help Tyrone feel better, perhaps by offering an apology or extending an invitation to Tyrone to play. Be cautious about demanding an apology, however. Some experts think children should not be forced to say things they're not ready to say. Still, planting the suggestion of an apology may start your child thinking about it.

Your child may also misinterpret the actions of other children. If, for instance, he is playing with others and someone accidentally pushes him, he may think he is being attacked. His instinct will be to protect himself. You can help him stop and think first. Teach him to recognize the push as an accident and to say to the other child, "That's okay," or "No problem." Learning to pay attention to how his behavior affects others and to pay attention to what the people around him are doing—in other words, learning to pay attention to social cues—is a valuable skill that will help your child not only in child care and in school but throughout his life.

Winding Down at Bedtime

Children who are active may look like they aren't ready for sleep, even when they're tired. In fact, being overtired can have the paradoxical effect of making children look even more active. Adrenaline may kick in to help a child who is overtired stay awake, so you may be seeing the effect of adrenaline rather than a child who is not tired. And this effect makes it even harder for a child to calm himself.

It may be tempting to let your child stay up until he looks more tired, but if he has difficulty stopping playing long enough to calm down, he'll need your help. Make a consistent bedtime routine, such as putting on pajamas, having a snack, brushing teeth, and reading or telling a story. Let your child know it's time to stop and unwind. If he protests, tell him, "You don't have to go to sleep right away, but you must lie quietly in your bed."

A very active child may also have trouble calming himself for naptime at home or at child care. As at bedtime, a consistent routine will help. Find out from your provider what her naptime routine is; you may be able to adopt some of the same preparations so that the routine will become a signal to your child that helps him calm down.

Try to make bedtime the same time every night. You may be tempted to keep a child who is active up a few minutes later, thinking he will sleep in the next day, but he more than likely won't. Instead, he probably will get up at the same time or earlier, and he's apt to be cranky if he didn't get enough sleep. Usually children will fall asleep fairly soon when they've had a busy day, when bedtime comes at a reasonable time, and when there's a consistent routine.

When to Get Help

It can be hard to determine when a child with a high activity level is outside of the norm. Follow the suggestions covered so far in this chapter for three or four months. Determine whether your child is still constantly in motion, is having difficulty sticking to an activity for more than a few minutes, is acting without considering the consequences, or is having difficulty following routines. For instance, a preschooler should be able to sit in a chair at the dinner table for a short time without crawling under it, falling off of it, or running around it. A preschooler can usually maintain interest in an age-appropriate television program without turning somersaults the whole time. A four-year-old can generally pay attention long enough to complete a twelve-piece puzzle.

If you're in doubt about your child's behavior, you should consult with your child care provider. Most providers have worked with so many children that they can help parents put their child's energy level in perspective. Your provider is apt to have a good idea whether your child is considerably out of the norm in his activity level and his ability to focus. If, after several months of working with him, your child is constantly in motion and distracted, it might be time to consult your health care provider or an early childhood assessment program. The important question is whether your child's activity level is interfering with his ability to learn the things he needs to learn and develop the social skills appropriate for his age.

Attention-Deficit/Hyperactivity Disorder (ADHD) gets a lot of press, so both parents and providers are likely to wonder whether this might be the problem. Children with ADHD are very distractible and impulsive, and they have excessive energy (hyperactivity), a level of excess energy that usually stands out and gets noticed by others. (ADD—Attention Deficit Disorder—is the same thing without the hyperactivity.) This diagnosis can't usually be made until a child is five or six years old, and then it must be made by a doctor or mental health professional. But it's important to realize that only about 3 to 5 percent of school-age children in the United States have either form of this disorder. It's also important to know that a child who has been exposed to violence or is suffering from post-traumatic stress disorder or an anxiety disorder can appear to have ADHD or ADD though he actually does not.

• • •

Points to Remember and Discuss

- Children's activity level usually peaks at around three or four years of age.

- A two-year-old can usually sit and pay attention for only two or three minutes. A five-year-old can often pay attention for ten or fifteen minutes.
- Children with unusually high activity levels are generally more noticeable in child care settings than they are at home.
- A child who is highly active needs lots of opportunities to run and tumble and move and burn off energy.
- For a highly active child, a calming environment may be better than a stimulating environment.
- Having a high activity level is a problem only when it gets in the way of a child's learning and socialization.
- Routine and calming activities around naptime and bedtime can help.
- ADHD and other high-activity disorders are unique and should be discussed with and diagnosed by a health care professional.

Chapter 6

Watch This!
Attention Getting

What's Normal

Positive attention is like food—it is absolutely essential to helping children grow. In the 1940s, a doctor named Rene Spitz did studies showing that orphans whose physical needs were met but who received no positive attention—basic nurturing such as hugging, cuddling, and comforting talk—simply failed to grow. Giving children positive attention is an important part of caring for them.

Children love to have adults spend time with them, notice the things they're doing, and comment on what they're learning. Some children seem to need more attention than others, and for busy parents, their children's demands for attention may feel insatiable. You're making dinner and your child is begging you to come play with her. You've finally gotten a chance to sit down and read the paper, but your child is saying, "Look at my picture," "Come see my puzzle."

You cannot always immediately stop what you're doing

and go look at the puzzle. While it's essential to respond in a supportive way when your child asks for attention, you can also help her take steps toward independence.

The amount of individual attention children get will be different at a child care center, at a family child care, and at home. A child care center has many children, usually grouped by age, and although the staff will try their best to give one-on-one attention, doing so can be difficult and much depends on the ratio of staff to children. A family child care setting usually has one provider but fewer children, and often children of more varying ages. Such a provider may have more flexibility to include your child in special tasks or otherwise give special attention, depending on how many children she cares for.

Although it seems like it should be easiest of all for your child to get special attention at home, this may not be the case. It may actually be harder for a parent to pay attention to a child throughout the day than it is for a child care provider. A parent who has been at work must then take care of the house and manage the details of life while also caring for his child. For the provider, watching the child is her job. Her days are usually organized entirely around caring for a group of children, while a parent must fit caring for his child into an already crowded day. Making time for your child is a considerable challenge. But there are many ways you can succeed at it, and many ways to coordinate your efforts with your provider.

Enjoying Your Child

One easy way to give your child attention is to take

pleasure in your child's pleasures. Children are excited about their accomplishments and newfound skills, and they want you to be excited too. Showing your enthusiasm helps to grow your child's self-esteem and his belief that he is a lovable person. This in turn helps to grow his confidence, and therefore his independence.

Let your child know of your pleasure by praising her. Your positive comments will be more effective if they are specific. "Look how you swirled the purple paint into such a nice pattern," or "I love how you lined up all your stuffed animals when you cleaned." You can help your child find pleasure in her own work by asking things like "Which part did you like the best?"

You can also show your excitement and pleasure in things your child brings home from child care, or encourage him to take things he is proud of to child care. Collect stories from your provider about what your child has done there, and comment on what you've heard about to your child. You can say something like "Mrs. Hedin told me you were a really good helper at snack time today."

You can also include your child in your work. Children love to help their parents. You might pull a chair over to the sink when you're peeling carrots and let your child wash the carrots for you. Your child can stand next to you and help wash the car with his own sponge. He can use his little broom to help sweep the kitchen, or hold the end of the tape measure when you're building something. Including him in your work satisfies a child's need for attention and makes him feel valued. Ask if your provider includes the children in daily tasks, like wiping the table after snack, setting the table, or helping with younger kids by, for example, bringing a baby her pacifier. Such activities not only are natural ways to show attention, but they also can instill confidence and teach responsibility.

If your child seems to brag or exaggerate in order to get your attention, he may need a confidence boost. Help him feel justly proud and confident by noticing his real, everyday accomplishments. Comment on times when he is strong or runs fast or makes good decisions or figures something out for himself. At the same time, avoid excess or false praise and making comparisons between children. Just focus on your child's accomplishment for its own sake, and de-emphasize competition.

Ask your provider if she has noticed your child bragging or exaggerating at child care. If she has, ask her to go out of her way in giving your child positive feedback.

Negative Attention

Sometimes children act out in order to get attention, especially if they realize they get more attention when they are misbehaving than when they're not. One signal can be when a child breaks a rule and then looks at you to see your reaction. Your provider may pick up on this more quickly than you do, especially if your child has been in the habit of doing this for a long time. You may be surprised if your provider calls this to your attention and wonder if she is mistaken, but try to take a step back and look at her feedback objectively. If you find that she

is right, you may need to make a conscious effort to
focus on giving your child attention before she asks for it
and on letting her know how much you appreciate her
good behavior.

When your child does break a rule, pay as little attention as possible. You should certainly respond, especially
if what she's doing is harmful or dangerous, but simply
tell her what she's doing is not acceptable, remind her
what to do instead, and then move her to another activity. It's best not to argue with her—especially if her arguing is an attempt to keep you involved with her. Instead,
let her know that you'll pay attention to her again when
she is behaving in a more helpful or respectful way. You
might say, "I will come and sit by you when you stop
kicking the table."

If your child often interrupts when other people are
talking, make a rule that only one person talks at a time.
You can say something such as "I'd like to hear what you
have to say, but someone else is talking. You need to wait
until Leah is done." You might allow her to tell you just
one word so you can both remember what she has to tell
you. Then be sure to ask her about it at an appropriate
time. Knowing such a rule could also help her at child
care, where there are many children who want to say
things. At the same time, be aware that young children
do not have endless patience and cannot wait too long. If
you're involved in a conversation with a neighbor and
your child is interrupting, you might ask her to wait until
you or your neighbor has finished the sentence. But then
say excuse me to your neighbor and listen to your child's

comment or question. Similarly, be sure when you pick up your child at child care that you give her your full attention rather than spending too much time talking with the provider.

Encouraging Independence

Sometimes children ask adults to play with them because they don't know how to get started themselves. Although playing with your child regularly is an important form of positive attention, you obviously can't be your child's playmate all the time. To encourage independent play on those occasions when you can't be his playmate, you might, for example, help your child choose a toy or an activity and spend a few minutes helping him get started. Let him know how long you will play with him. Once he is engaged in the play, comment on how busy he is, how independent he is. If he stops playing very quickly and begs you to play with him again, tell him lovingly but firmly that you have things you need to do right now but you will play with him again later. If he continues to ask you to watch him every two minutes, you can set limits on how many times you will watch him. You can say, "I will watch you one more time, and then I must do something else."

Make sure your child's toys are developmentally appropriate and in working order so they are appealing and useful. If his puzzles are too difficult, he won't attempt them. If they're too easy, he'll be bored and won't bother. Figures that are losing hair and missing parts won't be very appealing. Also, it's important that the toys, art materials, or other things your child usually plays with are stored where he can reach them.

Sometimes child care providers can give you good ideas about what toys and materials are appropriate for your child's age and level of development. Notice what kinds of toys and art materials your provider has and how she has them arranged. She may have good ideas for inexpensive, developmentally appropriate toys to purchase and good ideas for storing them in accessible ways at home. By the same token, if you've discovered something that your child remains engaged with for a sustained period of time, tell your provider about it. She may incorporate it in her environment or, if policy permits, allow your child to bring it from home and keep it in his cubby.

If you're feeling the stress of your child's constant need for attention, your provider probably is too. She will no doubt welcome a chance to share her insights and discoveries and to hear about yours.

Temperament and Cultural Differences

Children's temperaments are different. They simply arrive in the world with different natures and dispositions. Interestingly, culture also plays a part in influencing temperament. Chinese and Japanese cultures place a high value "on early mastery of self-control and on interdependence." Mothers in these cultures tend to "spend a lot of time holding and gently soothing their babies, who tend to be calm and quiet." American culture tends to value individuality and independence. European

American parents generally "use a more active and verbal parenting style," and their infants tend to be more active and talkative (Barbara Kaiser and Judy Sklar Rasminsky, *Challenging Behavior in Young Children: Understanding, Preventing, and Responding Effectively* [Boston: Allyn and Bacon, 2003]).

Similarly, different cultures within America, and different homes within those cultures, reflect different values about independence versus interdependence. So, too, there may be different expectations for independence between home and child care. For instance, you may carry your toddler longer than a child care provider would expect to do this. You may dress your child, whereas your provider normally expects her to be doing this for herself. Because your provider has many children to look after, she may ask your child to be independent more quickly. Try to be open to hearing her requests. She may not disagree with your way of doing something; it may simply be more difficult for her to help every child at the same level they are helped at home. Also be aware of letting her know what your child can and cannot do. If she wants your child to be more self-sufficient in putting on her coat, both of you may have to work together in teaching her this skill. On the other hand, your provider may be putting your child's coat on for her before every outing simply because she isn't aware that your child can do this.

Your child has come with her own genetically predisposed temperament into the culture of your specific home. You may wish her to be more independent, and you may be able to coach her in this direction. This doesn't mean you should push hard, however. Each child needs to be allowed to develop at her own pace. But you can give some encouragement toward independence. Here's one example. Tony had always craved a lot of attention, more than his brother and sister. It was sometimes hard for his mother to keep up with his requests. She worked full-time, and on weekends she seemed to have a million things to do. She decided to create a plan to help Tony entertain himself so she could get some work done.

When Tony was four years old, his mother told him she was going to have some quiet time every day when he would play by himself. Then Tony and his mother decorated a box and gathered toys that Tony was to use only during quiet time. They gathered magnetic letters and shapes and a cookie sheet to put them on, a puppet, books, large wooden beads to string, a yarn ball to toss, and tapes for his tape recorder. They set the box aside for Tony's special play-alone time.

Each day Tony and his mother went to his room, got out his special box, and put a tape in the recorder. Then his mother left the room and closed the door. Quiet time lasted for only a couple of minutes to begin with, but soon Tony was able to enjoy his play-alone time for ten minutes. (A three-year-old will probably be able to play alone for only five minutes, while a four-year-old can manage ten or fifteen minutes by himself, and a five-year-old can last for fifteen to thirty minutes.)

Tony's mother told her family child care provider

about the special box, and the provider asked if Tony could bring a similar box to child care. Tony had been having trouble with quiet time there also, repeatedly running into the kitchen when the provider was trying to clean up after lunch. The special box proved to be a boost for Tony at child care as well, helping to give him a bit of independence. This solution may not have been an option at a center, but center staff can address issues like this in their own effective ways if you keep them informed about your child's unique needs.

If Your Child Suddenly Asks for More Attention Than Usual

Sometimes children who know how to play alone at least some of the time suddenly change. They cannot be apart from you for more than two minutes at a time. They constantly ask you to do this, do that, come here, go there, and that is not the way they usually behave. If this happens with your child, think about whether something has happened recently that might be causing her stress. Have there been any changes at home? Talk with your provider and find out if she is seeing the same thing. Ask if anything has changed at child care recently. Has a new child started attending or is there a new teacher? Is your child having conflicts with someone there?

If you can locate the source of the stress, you may be able to do something to change it. Sometimes, however, the only thing you can do about the stress is to give your child the extra attention she needs. She may simply need the reassurance of your presence a little more often. Be sure to let your provider know if there are special stresses in your child's life. She then can also give your child some extra attention during this phase. And remember that it won't last forever. The extra time you put in now will pay dividends later when your child has negotiated the stress and feels secure again.

It's also possible that an increased need for attention has nothing to do with stress. Children move back and forth in their need for closeness to a parent. They repeat this cycle throughout their development. So an increased need for attention may simply be part of your child's normal development. The solution is simple: Just give your child the attention she or he needs.

• • •

Points to Remember and Discuss

- Children need attention to grow emotionally as well as physically.
- Children benefit from positive attention, such as noticing and praising their efforts and achievements and their good behavior.
- Children sometimes seek attention by acting out because negative attention feels better to them than no attention.
- Fostering independence can reduce a child's need for constant attention, but it doesn't help to push a child toward independence if the child isn't ready.
- A child's level of independence is also linked to her temperament and her culture.

- An increased need for attention might signal that your child is under stress, or it might be a normal developmental change.

Chapter 7
Want to Play Doctor?
Sexual Curiosity

What's Normal

Even young children are sexual beings. They may experiment with sexual play, from playing doctor to imitating adult behavior. They will certainly ask questions. "Where does the baby come out, Mommy?" "Do you have a penis, Mommy?" "Do you have babies, too, Daddy?"

Adults are often caught off guard by these questions, or by discovering their child involved in some kind of sexual play. What do you allow? How do you answer their questions? Do providers have the right to give information about sex to children? What if a provider finds your child involved in sex play with another child at the center? There are many different opinions about what is appropriate for children, about the age they should be to get certain information, and about at what age they should be allowed to participate in certain kinds of sexual activity. These differences are reflected in the controversy surrounding sex education programs in schools.

Whatever your feelings are about this issue, one thing seems clear: The most important thing in responding to your child's questions is to convey an acceptance of his curiosity as being natural.

An Up-Front Conversation with Your Provider

Some people are perfectly comfortable with their provider giving simple and clear answers to their children's questions about sex. Providers generally have a wealth of experience in this area, because they have heard so many questions from so many children. Still, some people prefer to handle all such questions themselves. It's important that you tell your provider if you want to be the person to answer these questions for your child. Ask her to tell your child that her question is a good question to ask her mommy or daddy.

In either case, you might ask your provider to let you know what kinds of questions your child is asking. This may prevent your being caught off guard when your child asks you the same questions. Also, ask your provider to tell you about any sexual play or exploration she finds your child involved in. She would in all likelihood do this in any event. Providers can, however, sometimes be so busy, and so accustomed to seeing these behaviors in children, that they fail to tell you about it. Let your provider know that you want to be kept informed.

Answering Their Questions

It's perfectly normal for young children to ask questions about sex, and it's important for adults to remember that their questions are very innocent. Young children tend to be interested in what people look like, how they are the same and how they are different. Do you and I both have the same things? Are our bodies alike? There are also questions that arise when a new baby is expected in the home. There are obvious changes in the mother's body, and there is often a flurry of activity and excitement about the house. This can produce all kinds of interesting and amusing questions or observations. For instance, two-and-a-half-year-old Katie was found putting the tip of a screwdriver into her belly button. When her very pregnant mother asked her what she was doing, Katie said, "I'm getting the baby out."

Convey an attitude of comfort and ease when you answer your child's questions about sex. You can lay the foundation for letting your child know that sex and intimacy are natural and wonderful human events. This doesn't mean you are encouraging early or inappropriate sex. In fact, you don't want to give more information than a child asks for. It only means that your manner and tone of voice when you answer do not suggest that sex is a bad thing in and of itself. The attitude you communicate may actually be more important than the explanation you give.

Give short, clear, accurate answers, and keep the lines of communication open for further discussions. Be sure to use correct terminology. Nicknames may lead to confusion. For example, when talking about body parts, use "penis," "scrotum," "vulva," "vagina," and "breast." You can also ask your provider to use correct terminology when talking to your child. Even if you do not want your provider to answer questions about sex, she probably will need to talk with your child about private body parts sometimes, such as when your child is using the bathroom, or if she should find your child involved in sexual play.

Too Much Information

Answer only what your child is asking about—don't provide more information than he asks for. When Katie's mother was pregnant, she was eager to be open about it and wanted to be sure Katie got correct information about childbirth. She got a book from the library that talked about penises and vaginas and planting the seed and birth canals. Katie let her mother know that she wasn't ready for that much information yet. Halfway through the book she climbed off the couch and began playing with her toys.

Sexual Play

While some information can be too much, most children are very curious about their bodies and how they compare to other children's bodies. A little boy may be very puzzled about where a little girl's penis went, and a little girl may be very curious about a little boy's penis and why she doesn't have one. They both need to know that girls have vulvae while boys have penises. And they need to know that both girls and boys are special in their own ways.

Many child care centers and family child care homes have anatomically correct dolls. If this isn't in conflict with your values, you may also wish to have such dolls at home. They provide one way for children to learn about differences in bodies. Books provide another way to explore and understand these differences. If your values are more conservative than your provider's, you'll need to have a frank discussion about any books and toys she uses that you don't want your child exposed to.

Don't be surprised should you find that your child and a visiting playmate have taken off their clothes so they can see their differences for themselves. When this happens, it's important not to give the children the message that they've done something bad. Accept their curiosity as natural. Say something like "You need to keep your clothes on when you play. Genitals are private and clothes keep them covered." Then redirect them to other types of activity. So that you can feel comfortable with how your child is being cared for, ask your provider how she handles it if she finds that children have undressed.

Masturbation

Some children have learned to comfort themselves by playing with their genitals or rubbing themselves on a toy or bedding. It also feels good to them. When this is done in private, it is rarely a problem. However, you will want to teach your child not to touch himself inappropriately in front of other people. Again, it is important not to shame your child. You might say something like "You've found it feels good to touch yourself. I'd like you to do that in private." You can also ask your provider if your child is doing this at child care and ask her to reinforce the message that what he is doing isn't bad but that it's private behavior.

Imitating Provocative Behavior

Children may try out provocative adult behavior, for instance, imitating the kissing, flirting, or provocative dancing they've seen. They also may seek attention by imitating the behavior. Let them know that they can get attention in other ways, and give them a simple message: "That looks like something grown-ups would do. Let's go do something else instead." This may be a heads-up for you to be more careful about the TV programs and movies your child is exposed to, either at home, at friends' houses, or even in a family child care setting. Talk to your provider about the TV shows she allows kids to watch and, if you suspect she is being too lax, be sure she understands your values and limits.

Good Touch/Bad Touch

Your child needs to be able to recognize inappropriate behavior and he needs to know that he has permission to say no. Sexual play between children of approximately the same age and size is normal and voluntary. But your child needs to know that big kids and adults should not touch his genitals or buttocks. Let him know that a doctor is an exception, and so are his parents or a child care provider if he needs help with cleaning himself or putting on medicine. Otherwise, let him know that he can say no. Tell him that if he's uncomfortable with play or with touch (sexual or otherwise), he can say, "I don't like that." He can leave the area. He can tell a grown-up. He can yell for help.

What If Something Doesn't Feel Right?

You may sense that something about your child's sexual play is wrong. Your child may imitate provocative adult behavior and keep on doing it or return to it even after you've told him that that's what adults do and have tried to divert him. You may find your child playing with another child in a way that is clearly adult, such as using tongues when kissing, or having oral genital contact. Or your child may simply seem more focused on sex than you would expect. Check with your child care provider to see if she is seeing the same things. You might also ask your child care provider if the amount of interest your child is showing in sex seems typical of the other children his age.

If your child seems to have an advanced understanding of sexual behavior or information, you need to figure out where this is coming from. Again, it may be from television and movies, and if so, you can be more careful about what he watches. Make sure that your provider is monitoring television watching closely as well.

If you believe your child could only have come to know sexual information by direct exposure to sexual activity, your child may have been or is being sexually abused. Think about where this could be taking place. Is your child ever alone with an adult or an older child? While sexual abuse sometimes occurs in a child care setting, it is very rare. It is actually more apt to occur with a friend or relative, difficult as this is to believe. If your child is being sexually abused, she needs your protection.

Indicators of sexual abuse include but are not limited to the following:

* experiencing pain or soreness in the genital area when walking, sitting, urinating, or defecating
* demonstrating adultlike sexual behavior
* being fearful of adults or certain individuals
* becoming extremely fearful of particular places or situations
* talking about or drawing sexually advanced information or behavior

Any of these behaviors could be caused by things other than sexual abuse. Sexual abuse is far from common, and sometimes people are too quick to assume that sexual abuse has occurred. Don't panic and jump to conclusions. If, however, you see a pattern of these behaviors and your concerns persist, it is important to take action. You can report your concerns to law enforcement or child protection services, and they can help you decide if there is adequate evidence to indicate abuse. You can also have your child assessed by a mental health professional who specializes in treating child sexual abuse.

• • •

Points to Remember and Discuss

* Children are full of curiosity about sex and naturally

experiment with sexual play, especially the how-are-you-different-from-me variety.

- You may wish to be the only person who answers your child's questions about sex, or you may be fine with your provider answering questions as well.

- You should convey an attitude of acceptance about your child's questions and sexual exploration while you teach her about privacy and appropriate limits.

- Children should not be given more information about sex than they ask for.

- Children need to be taught about what kind of touching is and is not appropriate.

- You need to be aware of the kinds of TV programs and movies your child is being exposed to.

- A child who is being sexually abused needs immediate attention and protection.

Chapter 8
I Am Telling the Truth:
Tall Tales and Falsehoods

What's Normal

Sean was three years old when he visited Walt Disney World with his parents. He saw Mickey and Minnie Mouse, Pluto, and Chip 'n Dale—adults dressed up in costumes and making the rounds entertaining the young children. The costumes had zippers down the back, and the heads could be lifted off. Sometimes you could see a bit of the adult's neck when the head separated from the rest of the costume.

Sean spied this anomaly in Mickey, Pluto, and Chip 'n Dale. "They're not real," he whispered to his father. "There are people inside them." He had not, however, spied this anomaly in Minnie's costume, and whispered with heartfelt joy to his father, "But Minnie is real."

Sean believed the evidence of his eyes. His brain could not yet think abstractly; he could not extrapolate the information that Minnie was a person in costume just as the other characters were. Did he tell the truth? No. Did he lie? No. Very young children can't lie. Their brains have not developed sufficiently to allow them to intentionally tell a lie. They might not tell the truth; they might say something that is contrary to fact. "There's a monster in my closet," or "Jimmy went to the moon yesterday" may not be truth as adults know it. But that doesn't mean such statements are intended to deceive.

Only when children reach the age of about three-and-a-half or so do they begin to acquire the skills that allow them to intentionally deceive. In order to lie, a child must be able to act calmly, think quickly, and talk about the abstract. Even then, much of childhood "lying" is a failure to distinguish between fantasy and reality. Sometimes children simply have forgotten. And sometimes they do intentionally lie. "I didn't do that." "I didn't put it there." "I already brushed my teeth." They lie in the service of self-protection.

This kind of behavior will appear both at home and at child care. Chances are your provider won't be overly concerned. If she's been doing this job awhile, she will have seen how normal it is in young children. Parents are more apt to be worried by this behavior. They may wonder what kind of child they're raising. If she lies when she's four years old, what will it be like when she's a teenager? When she's an adult? They may feel they need to be severe about the lying and nip it in the bud. Actually, it's much better not to react too strongly. The occasional lies of childhood neither predict poor character nor reflect poor parenting.

While it's important not to overreact, you can begin to help your child distinguish between truth and lies.

Here are some suggestions for doing that.

Confusion and Imagination

Rasheen comes home from child care and tells his father, "Jimmy flied in the park with his grandpa yesterday."

The father answers, "I know that's not true. People can't fly."

"Uh-huh," he insists indignantly. "Jimmy told me."

Jimmy might recently have been on an airplane with his grandfather and Rasheen got confused about the story Jimmy told him. Or maybe Rasheen watched *Peter Pan* and extended the story to Jimmy. Or Jimmy might really have gone with his grandfather to a place where helicopter rides are given. In this case, let's say Rasheen's father knew that Jimmy's grandpa was in town visiting, and he'd seen the two of them at the local park the afternoon before.

Rasheen's father could move into a power struggle with Rasheen, insisting that Jimmy had lied to him and that Rasheen was lying to his father. Or he could explain that only birds and machines can fly, that people must ride in airplanes if they're going to fly, and that Rasheen should not lie anymore. But probably none of this would make a lot of sense to Rasheen. Instead, his father could avoid the power struggle and try to understand the wish that underlies Rasheen's statement. He might simply say, "Wouldn't it be fun if people really could fly?" This suggests the difference between reality and fantasy without making any negative judgments or demanding a level of thought that Rasheen isn't yet capable of.

Your child may be working to understand the difference between real and pretend. Talk about that difference when you watch television or movies, read books, or talk about things others say. For example, another thing Rasheen's father could have said is, "Jimmy was having a lot of fun pretending he could fly."

Learn to appreciate your child's ability to tell enjoyable stories. You might ask him to tell you stories and write them down or tape-record them. Rasheen's father, for example, might have said, "That's a great story. Would you like to tell me a story about little boys who can fly whenever they want?" He might then offer to write down the story Rasheen tells. Such an activity encourages your child's imagination, and provides the opportunity to talk about the difference between real and pretend. "You have a wonderful imagination," you can say. "Look at all the things you made up in that story!" You could take one of your child's stories to child care and share it with your provider. She may wish to read your child's story to the group.

True and Not True

Along with learning the difference between real and pretend, children can begin to learn the difference between true and not true. A way to lay the foundation for honesty is to play a game suggested by Linda and Richard Eyre in *Teaching Your Children Values* (Fireside, Simon and Schuster 1993). This game is generally appropriate by the time a child reaches the age of four. If your provider hasn't heard about this game, tell her about it.

In this game, you make statements and then ask your child to say whether the statement is true or false. Start with simple things that your child can see. For example, you could say, "My shoes are brown." (True) "The grass is purple." (Untrue) "I am wearing green pants." (True) "My hair is green." (Untrue) Ask several more simple questions about things that are visible.

Then move to behaviors. "What if I pick up my toys and then I say my room is clean?" (True) "What if I don't pick up my toys and say my room is clean?" (Untrue) "What if I break a toy and tell a grown-up I did it?" (True) "What if I break a toy and say someone else broke it?" (Untrue)

You can build on this game by telling your child that when a person tells something that isn't true, it's called lying. You can say that lying is wrong and then talk about how important it is to tell the truth.

The Paul Bunyan Lie

In Chapter 6, we talked about a young child exaggerating his feats in order to get attention. This is relevant to our discussion of lying. Like the legendary Paul Bunyan, who could cut hundreds of trees with one swipe of his ax, your child might want to be bigger than life. Sometimes children will exaggerate to gain recognition.

Again, scolding your child about lying is not very helpful. It's better to help him feel proud and competent. Again, think about the wish that underlies the claim. Bolster his confidence by commenting on times when he really is strong, makes good decisions, or runs fast, for example. If he brags about being the fastest runner, even if you know it's not true, it's not helpful to say, "That's not true. John can run faster than you can." What's important here is that you recognize your child's need to be recognized. You can say something encouraging, such as "You get faster every time you practice," or "You have a lot of fun running, don't you?"

You can also be aware of whether you are fostering an atmosphere of competition. Avoid making comparisons between your child and another. If your child comes home from child care and says he climbed almost to the top of the jungle gym, don't ask questions such as "Did Johnny get all the way to the top?" or "Did you get higher than Johnny?"

You can also discuss with your provider whether she observes your child bragging or exaggerating more than other children his age. You may find that the exaggerating your child does is very typical. If, on the other hand, you learn that his exaggerating is more intense than that of other children his age, you can strategize with his provider about ways to reduce his sense of competition at child care as well as at home. Games focused on who can be first, best, or fastest are apt to foster competition. A game like "Beat the Clock," in which the child plays against the clock rather than against another child, might be preferable. Games like playing on tire swings or painting murals are likely to foster cooperation. If your child seems to brag a lot more than other children his age, ask your provider to focus for a while on giving him extra strokes and on having the children in her care play cooperative rather than competitive games.

Lying to Stay Out of Trouble

There are times when a child intentionally lies. This is the "I didn't do it" kind of lie. There's always the possibility that she really didn't do it, so don't automatically assume your child is lying. There will, of course, be times when you know she did it. In a child's mind, there are perfectly good reasons for not telling the truth. Telling lies to stay out of trouble doesn't suggest that your child is going to grow up to be a pathological liar. Such lies are normal; you don't have to worry. At the same time, you'll want to show your child that you value honesty.

Your child might want to conceal the truth so she isn't embarrassed. You might help her out by saying, "I see the juice is spilled. Please get a rag and wipe it up," rather than asking her if she spilled the juice.

Your child might be distorting reality to get what she wants. This is very typical for a young child. She may say "Yes" if you ask her if her room is clean, especially if she wishes this were true so she can please you. Again, you can help her out by reducing the temptation to lie. You can say, "Let's go see how you're doing cleaning your room," and then help her figure out how to finish the task. Teach your child to ask for help if a task is overwhelming.

Your child might be worried about punishment. Children are more tempted to lie when their parents or child care providers show a lot of anger when a child misbehaves. You can help your child with this by remaining relatively calm and by focusing on being fair when she misbehaves. She's more apt to own up to her misdeeds if she's not frightened of punishment. Children lie less often to people they respect and trust.

Children also worry about being "bad." They really want more than anything to please the adults they love. You can give your child lots of reassurance that she pleases you, that you think she's wonderful, and that you love her. And when she owns up to a misbehavior, you can praise her. Tell her how proud you are that she told you the truth.

If you sense that your child is lying to avoid punishment because she's afraid and you know that you are generally careful to remain calm when she's misbehaved, you might investigate how your provider handles similar situations. You may find that you and your child care provider hold different values regarding when a child is or is not telling a lie. Providers, like other people, may see anything that is not strictly factual as a lie; they may discount the idea that a child's imagination may be driving her story. If your provider sees it this way, it's also possible that she has a strong negative reaction to "lying." Discuss this, and if you cannot come to a better understanding, this particular setting may not be a good fit for your child.

Modeling Honesty

The most powerful teacher is the behavior you model for your child. This is true, too, for the provider. Children watch the important adults in their lives very carefully, and they mimic them. If Mom or Dad lies, the child is more apt to grow up thinking it's okay to lie.

Adults often lie without realizing it. Our "little white lies" are ubiquitous. Children can't tell the difference between an "acceptable" lie and a lie that is "wrong." For instance, your child might hear you tell your husband you don't like the new color of your neighbor's house. Then, when your neighbor asks how you like the new color, you avoid hurting his feelings by saying, "It's nice. I love it." Your child, who is still very literal, may interpret this as a lie.

Your child also may watch adults exaggerate their accomplishments. Fish stories are so classic that we take them in stride without condemning the teller. Sometimes adults exaggerate their stories because they're getting a good laugh, and they like entertaining people. Whatever it is, your child is apt to pick up on it. So be aware of your own words.

• • •

Points to Remember and Discuss

- The brains of very young children have not developed sufficiently to allow them to intentionally tell a lie.
- Children do not have the skills to intentionally deceive until they reach the age of about three-and-a-half and can act calmly, think quickly, and talk about the abstract.
- The occasional lies of childhood neither predict poor character nor reflect poor parenting.

- You can help a child sort out the difference between reality and fantasy by labeling certain statements as pretend, but do so without judgment.
- Children sometimes exaggerate their feats to get attention, and this tendency may increase when competition is encouraged.
- Children may lie to stay out of trouble, especially if an adult gets very angry or punishes them.

Chapter 9
You Can't Make Me:
Power Struggles

What's Normal

Toddlers are working on the developmental task of gaining autonomy. A child this age is struggling to understand and prove that she is a person separate from her mother or father. This is one of the reasons children this age are so determined to proclaim, "No," or "I can do it myself." While the struggle for autonomy is most intense at the toddler stage, preschoolers continue to work on this task.

Children need chances to do things for themselves and to make their own decisions, both of which lead to healthy independence. But their assertions of independence can lead to power struggles as well. What parent hasn't wanted to take over the buttoning when the family's late for an event? What parent hasn't insisted a child stop playing immediately and clean up? It's time to go. And the child digs in his heels and cries or screams and simply refuses to pick up. The parent thinks, "I can't back down now. How else is he going to learn?" And a power struggle ensues. But there are ways to stop these kinds of power struggles before they start.

Children need limits. Limits help them feel safe. The only problem is that they don't yet understand this, so they resist limits, and a power struggle may ensue. Even when your child seems totally bent on fighting with you, however, you can enforce the limits and step out of the fight.

Temperament plays a part in how apt a child is to engage in a power struggle. Some children have a greater need to exert control than others do. Such children can present a great challenge to the patience of a parent or a child care provider, and caring for them may require extra coordination between parent and provider. People often think of such children as stubborn. There is another way to think that might help you feel some sympathy for your child and get less caught up in a power struggle. You can think of him as working hard on his independence, which is a worthy goal.

No matter what temperament your child has, you need to help your young child develop both independence and cooperation. The following sections describe things you and your child care provider can do to increase the chance that your young child will follow directions and accept limits without a power struggle.

"No" as the Default Setting

"No" comes out of the mouths of toddlers and some young preschoolers before they even think about it. It's automatic. They don't necessarily mean it when they say no, which can feel very confusing to parents and child care providers. Have you ever asked your child if she wants juice, only to have her say no and then cry when you don't give it to her? Saying no may simply be a habit for your child. It may make her feel powerful. It may give her a sense of having some control.

There are some simple ways to avoid getting caught on this crazy merry-go-round. One way is to ask questions that cannot be answered with a no. For example, you can show her the container of juice and ask, "How much juice do you want?" You can also find ways to let her be independent by giving her choices, such as deciding what to play, and letting her do many things for herself.

Another strategy is to model saying "yes" for her. Avoid using the word "no" whenever you can. You might say, "Yes, when the toys are cleaned up," or "Yes, you may, after you're done." Tell your child what to do instead of what not to do. Instead of saying, "No, don't run in the hallway," say, "Please walk in the hallway."

If you think your child is in the no-as-default-setting stage, ask your provider to make a conscious effort to use the word "yes" with her more often. Providers generally are quite aware of young children's tendency to go with an automatic no, but they are attending to many children. Your provider may appreciate hearing a respectful request to say yes as often as possible.

Taking Preemptive Actions

There are various reasons children don't follow directions. Maybe they aren't sure how to do what you've asked, or maybe the job is too big for them. "Clean your room" can be a big request for a three- or four-year-old. To help avoid a power struggle, be clear and concrete about what you're asking. Keep directions simple. A young child can grasp only one- or two-part directions. So you might say, "Put your blocks away, and then put your books on their shelf."

Make sure, too, that your child is paying attention and hears you. You might kneel down, talk directly to him, and ask him to repeat your directions. This helps him remember what you want him to do. You can also make sure he knows it's all right to ask for help. Your provider can do the same, giving clear directions about carrying the spoons to the lunch table and putting them at each child's place.

Sometimes children fail to follow directions because they're having too much fun playing. Even adults find it hard to stop doing something that's fun and switch to a chore they know needs doing. So be patient. Warn your child when it's almost time to put away toys or change activities. You can also remind him that his coloring book will be there when he comes back and he'll get to finish his picture then. Give him incentives. For example, let him know that when he's hung up his coat he can play a game. Try to arrange your schedule so you can arrive at child care early enough to let your child switch gears to going home, allow perhaps a couple of minutes for extra play.

Giving choices also can help you sidestep power struggles. Try to set up situations that give your child a choice. You might say, "Do you want to do it yourself, or shall I help you?" Sometimes he may welcome your help. Sometimes your question might spur his independence, and he'll want to do it himself. At such a time, you can support his initiative and offer suggestions to help him be successful. Other examples of choices are "What do you want to pick up first, your books or your blocks?" "Do you want to wear the red sweater or the blue?" "Do you want to come now or in two minutes?"

Disengaging from the Argument

Sometimes a child will argue even after you've set a very firm limit. She asks for ice cream just before lunch and you say no. But she just keeps at you and at you. You can simply withdraw from the argument, repeating to yourself the old adage "It takes two to argue." Or you can say something like "You're trying to get me to change my mind, but I'm not going to. You need to stop asking now." Then ignore her pleas.

It is amazing what disengaging can accomplish. For example, the provider at a child care center was in the kitchen dishing up a plate of apples and cheese for snack when she heard a terrible noise from the classroom. Hurrying there, she found that Timmy had overturned Jesse's chair while Jesse was sitting on it. Timmy insisted it was his chair. The provider pointed out to Timmy that Jesse had already been sitting in that chair, but there was an empty chair on the other side of the table. Timmy stood in the corner and refused to come to the table. He said, "But that's where I always sit." The provider said,

"No one has a special chair here. You need to sit in an empty chair." Then she ignored his continued protests. The next day, of course, Jesse made sure he got to that chair before Timmy did, but this time Timmy simply took a different chair.

Even when they know they shouldn't, parents sometimes give in to their children simply because it's easier. Maybe they're just plain tired—or perhaps they feel guilty. Although it may take more work and resolve not to give in to your child at times, it's usually worth it in the long run. Especially if it's an important issue, make your decision about what your child is asking based on what is best for her in the long run—not on what's easier at the moment. Don't give in just to get your child to stop begging or arguing.

It's also okay to change your mind if you make a hasty decision and then realize your "no" was unnecessary. Maybe your child is so hungry it's really hard for her to wait another half hour, and she's asked for a snack. Your first instinct is that it's too close to lunch. Then you realize it's been a long time since she's eaten and a small snack probably won't keep her from eating lunch. You could then say, "I thought about that a bit more, and I changed my mind. I know you're especially hungry right now, and I'm sure an apple won't ruin your lunch."

Sometimes children are really good at arguing because they've found it's a way to get attention. If your child argues a lot, try paying extra attention to him when he's not arguing. Comment on the times when he's cooperative. Let him know how much you like it when he does what you've asked him to do or listens when you say no.

Picking Your Battles

If your child's temperament is such that he constantly pushes for independence and you find yourself repeatedly drawn into power struggles, you may have to decide which battles are worth fighting. If your child argues about everything endlessly, you need to pick your battles. Hold your ground only on important things. For instance, if it's cold outside and your child refuses to wear a coat, you may need to hold your ground. No coat, no outside. But maybe your child insists she's going to wear a pair of pants with a hole in the knee. Depending on what you're doing that day, this may not be a big deal. Pay attention to your reactions and see if your own rigidity might be contributing to unnecessary power struggles.

Consult with your child care provider to find out if she sees your child as particularly challenging in pushing limits and refusing to comply with requests and directions. Because she sees so many children, your provider can give you an important perspective on your child. You might find out that your child is typical and that you may be holding unrealistic expectations. Or you may learn that your provider is struggling too. Strategize together so that you present consistent expectations.

Discussions with your provider may disclose serious differences in your approaches to discipline. Usually, if you discuss these differences openly, you'll be able to find ways to work together in the best interest of your child. If, however, your provider insists on continuing to follow practices that are in conflict with your beliefs and values, even after you've expressed concern, you may want to find a setting where approaches to dealing with power struggles and other discipline issues are more flexible and compatible with yours.

Leah was an I-can-do-it-myself kind of girl. When she was only two years old, she climbed into the bathroom sink so she could explore the medicine cabinet. She also climbed on top of the piano to get at photographs she found interesting. When she was three, she assured her older brother that she could open the door he was having difficulty with. And she did. When her child care provider would ask Leah to hurry so everyone would get across a street while the light was still green, Leah would look at her and slow down to baby steps. Her child care provider told her mother that Leah was one of the most "stubborn" children she'd ever cared for.

Fortunately, the provider enjoyed Leah and saw that her "stubbornness" also was a strength. The provider and Leah's mom kept in close contact, and both focused on giving her lots of opportunities to do things for herself. They appreciated her ingenuity and praised her whenever she was cooperative. What could have been a trait that resulted in endless power struggles was celebrated as determination, and Leah learned that there were times she could have her way and times she couldn't.

If you have a particularly determined child, you and the provider will no doubt need support from each other. You may find that your child frustrates you both to the limit. A little empathy from the other adult who cares for this child can go a long way toward helping both of you cope. Give your provider encouragement and support, and be open to receiving encouragement and support from her. Let your provider know if something she's doing seems to be helping your child do less pushing against your limits. And don't hesitate in asking her opinion about things she sees you doing.

There are times when a child's behavior goes beyond refusing requests. It may become so disruptive that it upsets the child care setting. Such a child might have difficulty controlling anger, constantly seek attention in negative ways, have severe tantrums, or purposely do the opposite of what he or she is asked to do. If this is the case with your child, you may want to see a counselor.

• • •

Points to Remember and Discuss

- Children often say "no" because they need to show that they are independent, separate individuals.
- Some children have a greater need to control their environment than others do.
- The same child might be seen as stubborn or as determined, depending on the attitude of the caregiver.
- You need to model use of the word "yes."
- You should avoid asking questions that call for "yes" or "no" answers.
- You should give your child choices.
- Cooperative behavior should be praised.

- You should look for ways that your child can be powerful.
- Power struggles can be sidestepped by offering limited choices and giving plenty of warning.
- You can call an end to an argument.
- Every battle is not worth winning; choose to hold the line only on the important ones.

Chapter 10
I'll Kick and Scream until I Get My Way:
Temper Tantrums

What's Normal

Temper tantrums can be unsettling for parents and providers alike. It helps to know that tantrums are normal for toddlers and young children. When children get frustrated by their inability to do something they're trying to do, or are refused something they really want, they may have a full-fledged outburst, kicking, crying, screaming, throwing things, banging about, and throwing themselves to the floor. A somewhat older child may shout, scream, cry, and stomp about instead of throwing himself on the floor and kicking.

While normal, tantrums are uncomfortable for both adults and for the children who are having them. Children don't generally like to feel so out of control, and they may become anxious about their overwhelming feelings. You and your provider can help your child learn coping skills so he isn't so quick to resort to tantrums. It's also important to give children support when they do lose control, first by containing them and then by helping them to calm themselves and return to a comfortable state.

Your child will learn coping skills more easily and more quickly if you and your child's provider are on the same page. You can talk over with your provider the issues described below. Be sure, too, to let her know about any particular frustrations or situations that trigger temper tantrums for your child.

Arsenic Hour

Adults may respond to children's temper tantrums with fear or anger. It can be overwhelming to an adult as well as to a child to be confronted by such out-of-control behavior. You might start thinking, "He's so out of line. I won't tolerate this kind of behavior," and begin yelling yourself. Understanding why your child has temper tantrums should help you. Above all, don't take it personally. Remember that temper tantrums are normal behavior for young children.

Exhaustion, illness, and hunger can all trigger tantrums. Think how much harder it is for you to remain calm and reasonable at the end of a long day when you are bone tired, or at the end of the workday when you're ravenous and dinner isn't ready yet. If you feel this way, your child probably feels it doubly. Children have a lot of difficulty moderating themselves, and if they are hungry, tired, or sick, they are much more apt to lose control.

A little planning will go a long way toward avoiding tantrums. Pay attention to how often your child needs to eat, and plan meals and snacks accordingly. If he is unusually hungry, give him something to eat. This is one type of trigger to let your provider know about. If your child is particularly vulnerable to tantrums when he's hungry, it will help your provider to know she has to be especially watchful of this with your child. Children who are going through growth spurts can be hungrier than usual. If you notice this about your child, mention it to your provider so she can be aware that he needs something extra.

If he's unusually tired, you might have to change your plans for the day. If it's a child care day and your child did not sleep well the night before, let your provider know. If it's a small family child care, she may be able to delay an outing until the following day. Even if she can't rearrange the outing, at least she'll know your child needs extra attention. Rearranging schedules can be even harder in a large child care setting, simply because there are usually more children to be attended to and schedules are less flexible. Nevertheless, your provider might be able to make some accommodations. If your child is particularly tired, she can allow him to do less taxing activities or perhaps she can let him ride in the wagon or stroller if a field trip involves a lot of walking.

Plan your outings and challenging activities for times of the day when your child is full of energy, probably in the morning or in the afternoon after naptime. If your provider tells you that your child is having tantrums when they go on outings, find out what time of the day they go. Just before lunch or naptime or late in the afternoon all tend to be difficult times of the day for children. Just before the evening meal—a time that's often referred to as arsenic hour—may be the most difficult time of all. Providers generally will not plan outings during these times, and you should pay attention to these times at home as well.

Avoid complicated activities and instructions during times of the day that are difficult for your child. If, for instance, your child is on the verge of falling apart already, you probably don't want to tell him to get his socks off the laundry table in the basement, bring them to his bedroom, and put them in his drawer. Wait until after he's had something to eat. Similarly, you may be tempted to stop for one quick errand on your way home from child care. Although running into the pharmacy for aspirin sounds like a simple task, facing an extra errand at this time of the day may stretch your child beyond his capacity to cope.

Too Much Frustration

Children also tend to have temper tantrums when they're frustrated. You can help head off such tantrums by stepping in when you see that your child is about to be overwhelmed by frustration. If your child is working on a puzzle that you know is way beyond her ability, bring out an easier one. If she's trying to tuck in the flap of an envelope and you see she's about to tear up the envelope in frustration, offer to help. Better yet, offer to help before she gets to the point of tearing the paper. Again, tell your provider if there are particular toys or activities that frustrate your child quickly and that seem to trigger temper tantrums.

Look for opportunities to teach your child to recognize her feelings and, according to her age and developmental level, to use her words to express them. To a four-year-old, you might say, "It looks like you're getting frustrated and could use some help. It's easier if you ask for help; you can say, 'I'm having a hard time. Will you help me?'" You can teach your child other coping mechanisms to deal with her frustration, such as taking a break, changing activities to something that is less challenging and more fun, or taking a few big breaths.

The Sincerest Form of Flattery

Young children learn more from what you do than from what you say. If you have emotional outbursts in front of your child, he'll probably learn this behavior. If you scream when you're frustrated, so will your child. If you demand that your child come here now, your child is more apt to make the same kinds of demands. Being asked to change our own behavior in order to teach our children something different may be the biggest challenge of all. Accomplishing it may require getting some extra support. Still, it is essential. Recognize your own need to take a break. Use words to name your own feelings. Demonstrate how to calm down by listening to music, looking at a book, singing, drawing, or doing something fun.

If children learn behavior from watching their parents, they also learn from watching their child care

provider and other children at child care. Ask your
provider if there are children at child care who seem to
be having a hard time and are having a lot of temper
tantrums. If this is the case, visit with her about how she
manages. Ask her if she is getting a chance to let the
other children, including yours, know that the child who
is having the tantrums is simply having a hard time and
then can divert the other children to another activity.
Notice, too, if your provider or any of the staff at a center
regularly raises her voice or otherwise becomes overly
emotional when becoming frustrated with a child. If so,
talk about this candidly with your provider and express
your concern and the ideas we've discussed about how
adults can contribute to children's tantrums.

Not Rewarding Temper Tantrums

In the previous chapter we talked about setting limits
and picking your battles. If you've said no regarding
something that is important, something that is worth
fighting about, then don't give in to your child's tantrum.
Giving in when he has a tantrum teaches him that it
pays to kick and scream until he gets his way. It will also
make life more difficult at home and in the child care
setting, not only for you and your provider, but for your
child as well.

If your child is in the throes of a temper tantrum and
seems unreachable, don't try to reason with him. Don't
try to explain or cajole. Disengage, focus on something
else, or walk away. Ignore the outburst. When the
tantrum starts to abate, offer him comfort. Resist the

temptation to lecture. It won't help. Don't ask him to explain himself. He can't. Very few children have either the verbal skill or the ability to understand their own behavior enough to explain it. Their brains have not developed yet to a level where they can reflect on their behavior to any significant extent. Just help your child to move on and get involved in another activity.

Making Sure No One Gets Hurt

Sometimes children will get so out of control that they may hurt themselves or someone else. A flailing child can hit someone else or bang her body against a sharp corner or knock breakable things off a shelf and get cut. If your child is in danger of hurting herself, you may need to move things out of her way, or you may need to contain her. A gentle bear hug or rocking and gently stroking your child can help to contain her. Try to keep your own breathing calm to help calm her. If holding her seems to make it worse, let go. You want to be support-ive, not punitive. And remember, you can't help your child calm down unless you are calm yourself. If you are very upset, your child will experience anything you do or say more as punishment than as support, so take time to calm yourself first.

At home or at a child care center, other children may need to be moved out of the way of the child who is hav-ing the tantrum. Otherwise, she may end up lashing out or knocking into another child and hurting him. If this happens, you (or the provider) need to attend to the child who was hurt, tell him you're sorry it happened, and be careful not to blame in any way the child who's having the tantrum. Generally a larger center will have two staff members with a group of children, so one of them can stay near the child having the tantrum while the other staff person can divert the remaining children. In a smaller family child care, the provider probably can divert the other children while continuing to remain relatively near the child who's having the tantrum.

To repeat, remain calm, stay near your child when she's having a tantrum but remain disengaged, and sit near her when she stops the tantrum. When she's ready, help her restore order to anything that got knocked out of place during the outburst, and help her get started in another activity. Some children want to be held and comforted after a tantrum. Some don't. Respect your child's choice.

When a Temper Tantrum Lasts Too Long

Young children sometimes get locked in a temper tantrum. They simply don't know how to get themselves out. If your child has a tantrum that goes on for more than ten or fifteen minutes, you may need to move in close and tell him you know he's upset. Then say, "It's time to stop now." Help him take deep, relaxing breaths. If you're concerned that your child is having temper tantrums more often than most children do, check with your provider to find out if he's having frequent tantrums at child care as well, and ask your provider if she thinks his tantrums are more frequent or severe than those of other children. Make sure neither of you is giving into him because he has tantrums, but at the same time, try to take preventive steps. Monitor his environment closely to see that he is getting enough attention, sleep, and food, and is not being frequently frustrated by tasks that are beyond his ability. Check with your provider to see if she thinks he is getting enough attention and rest at child care as well.

If nothing works and your child's tantrums continue to be very frequent or very long, say several times a day for more than ten or fifteen minutes each time, you may wish to get an assessment from a mental health professional who specializes in working with young children. The same goes for a child who's so out of control that he tries to hurt you or others who try to help him. You'll want to schedule regular conversations with your provider to be sure your responses to tantrums are consistent and so you can keep track of their frequency and severity. You might ask your provider to count how many tantrums your child is having so you'll know if you're making progress in teaching him coping skills. If he was having four tantrums a day and now is having a tantrum only once a day, you and your provider can give each other a pat on the back.

• • •

Points to Remember and Discuss

- Temper tantrums are normal for young children.
- Children feel uncomfortable when they're having temper tantrums.

- Adults need to help children avoid the triggers of tantrums—hunger, exhaustion, illness, and frustration.
- Older children need to be taught to use their words to ask for help when they're frustrated.
- A child should not be rewarded after a temper tantrum.
- Adults need to monitor the environment so no one gets hurt during a tantrum.
- After a tantrum, a child should be helped to move on, without lectures or questions.
- Adults must be careful not to model out-of-control behavior.

Chapter 11
I Want to Play Too:
Joining a Group of Players

What's Normal

Young children don't know a lot about playing together. Until they're around two-and-a-half to three, they're in their own world, the one where they develop the physical and cognitive skills that eventually allow them to interact and communicate with other children. Toddlers start out with what's called parallel play. In other words, they play in the same space with the same toys, but they play alongside each other rather than together. As they get a bit older, they begin to watch one another and share ideas and toys; this is called associative play. At about the age of four or five they can begin to engage in pretend group play. This is when they begin to engage in real, cooperative play. Even by the age of three, however, children generally like the idea of having a friend. The word becomes important to them, even if they don't necessarily know what to do with a friend.

Children learn to play with others by first playing with you. By the age of four, many children are highly

motivated to join a group of children who are playing
together. They watch and they copy what the other children are doing. In some ways it's like learning to talk.
Many children don't have to be specifically instructed in
this skill. They are keen observers and they learn without
formal lessons.

A child's temperament influences how quickly she
moves in and out of play with others and how quickly
she learns social skills. Your child may be very outgoing,
quite shy, or somewhere in between. Wherever she is on
the continuum, she can probably benefit from an occasional bit of help in learning social skills. But you don't
need to push. Children also enjoy playing alone, and
when this is their choice, it's important to respect it.

Child care provides an ideal setting for children to
learn social skills. It gives children abundant opportunities to learn about cooperation and playing with others.
Another benefit of child care is the chance it gives you to
learn new things about your child. Your child care
provider can give you a lot of information about how easily your child joins in play with others and how she inter-
acts with them. Because she always sees your child in the
presence of groups, she may know even more than you do
about how easily your child is able to join in with other
children. But it's not a one-way street. You can give your
child care provider important information on how you've
seen your child develop in this area with the children of
friends, relatives, and neighbors. Together, you can
encourage and foster this important social skill of joining
in play with another child or with groups of children.

Giving Your Child a Boost

Watch to see if your child needs help in playing with other children. Perhaps when you're at a park, at a community center, or with a group of friends and their children, you notice that your child isn't joining the others. If you have any concerns about your child's ability to join in the play of other children, you might ask your provider if you could come watch her in her child care setting as well. Sometimes your child will not join in play with a group because at that particular time or with that particular group, she simply isn't interested. That's fine. She feels like playing alone. But if you notice your child hovering, looking upset, or always on the outside of play, you can offer her some help.

Your provider may notice more quickly than you do if your child is a bit shy or is struggling in some way to learn how to join other children in play. Let your provider know that you really want to hear about how your child is doing in this area. If your provider approaches you with a concern, try to be open to what she's saying. The concern she brings you may surprise you. It may make you uncomfortable. But it doesn't mean that there is anything wrong with you or your child. It may mean that your child is progressing at a different pace developmentally. Or it could just mean that your child needs a boost and you and your provider need to work together to help her.

One thing you can do at home to help your child practice cooperative play is to play with her yourself. Usually children who have a good relationship with other children also have a good relationship with the important adults in their lives. If you can, make time each day for some playtime together. Get down on the floor so you are at your child's level, and follow her lead. Let her direct the play scenario. Encourage her interest in developmentally appropriate toys and activities that lend themselves to cooperative play, toys such as blocks, or activities such as pretend games—playing house or store or school, for example.

You can also encourage your child by inviting playmates to your home. You might ask your provider to recommend a child who seems well matched with yours, someone your child plays with at child care who has a similar temperament and interests, perhaps. The first time a child visits in your home, be sure to allow her time to explore and feel comfortable. You can set up activities that your child and her friend can play together and may be familiar with from child care, such as fingerpainting or playing with puppets. Stay close enough so you can help them weave their play together. For instance, if your child is cooking and her friend is making a house, you could suggest something that links those two activities, such as having the child who's cooking take her neighbor some dinner. To help them keep it going, you may even want to join their play for a while. Just be sure to keep in mind that your role is to facilitate their playing together.

Helping Your Child Get In

If you notice that your child continues to have trouble

getting into a group, help her learn how to become part of the play. You might draw her attention to what the group is doing so she can imitate their actions. For example, if the other children are feeding grass to plastic dinosaurs, hand her some grass and suggest she feed her dinosaur too. If the other children bring their trucks or cars to the park to play in the sand, help your child choose one of her trucks to take to the park. Then, if the other children are loading a dump truck with sand, get down on the ground and help your child start loading her truck with sand. If she has an idea that fits with their play—say she wants to empty her truck in a new place to build a pile of sand—help her make the suggestion to another child. To help ensure that someone is paying attention, teach your child to say the name of one of the children before she makes her comment. This increases the chances that her idea will be acknowledged. She could say, "Tony, let's haul the sand to make a sand hill."

If you're in a setting with your child where groups of children are playing together, perhaps at a community center or a house of faith or with extended family, notice if there is an activity going on that seems to interest your child. Say, for example, that five children are playing school. Maybe you can give your child a prop to help her enter the play. Perhaps you could give her a notebook and pencil to take to the "classroom." Or help her join the play by pretending to be someone who fits into the scene. If one child is already the teacher, your child may need to claim a student role. Or perhaps she could be a mother who comes to pick up one of the children.

You can also talk with your provider about what she does to help your child get involved in playing with others. A formal child care setting usually has carefully designed environments with play areas that encourage different kinds of learning and interactions, such as dramatic play areas with props and toys to encourage imaginative group play. Children are often drawn to these areas to join others in playing pretend games during free time. Although a family child care setting may not have formal dramatic play areas set up, children undoubtedly get involved in pretend games of various kinds there as well. It only takes a cape to get a child started playing magician or superhero. If you have dress-up clothes at home that you're not using, ask whether your child and the others could use them as additional props for breaking the ice. You could also ask your provider to pay special attention to helping your child join these games and that she try using the types of techniques suggested above if she's not familiar with them.

You could also ask your provider if there are small group activities she could set up that would help your child learn to join in the play of others more easily. You might say, "My child loves the idea of having friends, but she doesn't always know how to connect with another child. I would appreciate your suggestions for small group games the children could play that might help her connect more easily." Examples of small group activities might include playing a board game such as Candy Land or coloring pictures at a table together or playing with playdough.

Stepping on Toes

Maybe you have a child who has no difficulty approaching groups of children. Perhaps she rushes right in, but she gets rejected. Sometimes children have difficulty joining others in play because they do it in a way that is disruptive. They haven't yet figured out how to join an existing group by fitting in. Instead, they want to move in and play their own game. For instance, a child who charges with a fire truck into a group of children who are rocking babies to sleep or playing house is likely to be rejected.

Some children try to bulldoze their way into groups. They think they can get other children to play by slapping their shoulders or karate kicking or tackling. Other children tend to reject such a child's overtures. If this description fits your child, try giving her some coaching. Say, "Why don't you try asking Mai if she wants to help you fix cereal for your doll?" You can also interpret your child's actions for the group by saying something such as "I think she's trying to squeeze into this spot to join your game." Check with your provider to find out if your child is too aggressive at child care when she tries to join groups. If your provider isn't sure, ask her to pay special attention for a few days and let you know. Your provider may see this kind of behavior before you do, since she regularly sees your child with others. She's likely to have helpful suggestions for you to use when this happens at home.

Sometimes children use bumps and kicks and pokes to get into groups because their verbal skills are limited.

If this is true for your child, it might be helpful to suggest that she assume nonspeaking roles in dramatic play, such as playing the person busing dishes at the restaurant rather than the waiter, or pretending to be the family pet. Ask your provider if she thinks limited verbal skills are contributing to your child's difficulty entering groups. Both of you can continue to offer suggestions for working with your child, with the understanding that if something doesn't work, you'll think of something else.

Keep checking in with your provider so you can let each other know what kind of progress your child is making on this front, both at home and in child care. But again, don't push your child too hard to play with groups of children. Some children love playing with lots of children much of the time, while others are happier with just one special friend or a few friends. And all children want some time to play alone.

When Difficulties Persist

Shy children sometimes stay on the outskirts of play. But if your child is four years old or more and continues to remain on the outskirts even when she knows the other children, it's possible that her hesitancy is about something other than shyness. You might consider if her language skills are age appropriate, her motor skills are insufficiently developed, or she doesn't understand pretend play. Consult with your provider regarding these questions. Many child care providers, especially if they've had specialized training, will have valuable perspectives; they work with many children your child's age. You might also consider getting a developmental screening done by your health care provider or school district.

• • •

Points to Remember and Discuss

- Children of different temperaments will find it more or less easy or difficult to join groups of children in play.
- Children play alone or engage in parallel play until they are developmentally ready for cooperative play, usually around the age of four.
- An adult can teach a child cooperative play skills by playing with the child.
- You can make suggestions for roles a child can take on during an existing group's playtime.
- You can give your child props, such as a doll or a truck or some other toy, to help her join a group.
- Limited verbal skills may lead a child to initiate play with aggressive physical moves. This approach is likely to lead to rejection.

Chapter 12
It's Mine, Mine, Mine:
Taking Turns

What's Normal

Arriving at child care at her customary time to pick up her son, Ahmed's mother was surprised when her family child care provider asked if she would give her a call that evening. She was both surprised and disturbed when the provider told her Ahmed seemed to be having a lot of trouble sharing. That morning he'd grabbed a rattle from an infant, and he'd had a full-fledged tantrum when his turn with a coveted computer game was over. The provider wanted to brainstorm with her about how they could help Ahmed accept sharing and taking turns.

Ahmed's mother was single and Ahmed was her only child. She didn't often see him in situations where he had to share. If she'd had additional children, she probably would have noticed his resistance to sharing. It's a behavior that parents of more than one child, as well as providers, see regularly.

Challenges with sharing and taking turns are more

apt to show up in child care settings, where children must interact with lots of other children, where there are more children competing for toys, and where children compete for the provider's attention. This means it's very possible that you might hear from your provider that she's having challenges with this issue before you are aware of it. Though it may be a surprise to you, try to remain open to what she has to say. It doesn't mean there's anything wrong with your child. Rather, your child is going through a natural developmental stage and has some skills he or she needs to learn.

Before the age of three and a half or four, many children are not developmentally ready to share. They may hoard materials or refuse to take turns. They may walk away when told they have to share, or grab things that others are using. This behavior persists even as they reach the age when they begin to be developmentally ready to share. Learning to share requires a great deal of adult guidance and lots of practice. Sharing doesn't come naturally. Children need adults to help them learn to give up toys or materials when they are done with them, to ask permission to use toys or materials, or to wait for a turn.

Chances to Practice

Ahmed was barely three and a half, and he was only beginning to be ready to share. The provider reassured his mother that she didn't need to be worried about him. His behavior was very typical of children his age, but there were things she could do to help him learn how to share.

His mother introduced the idea of taking turns into her play with him. On weekends, while Ahmed was fresh and full of energy, his mother played games with him that had a back-and-forth rhythm. They would roll toy cars back and forth or they would roll a ball back and forth. She would say "my turn" when the ball reached her, and "your turn" when it reached Ahmed. This emphasized the idea of turns to Ahmed. Another game she tried was to talk on a toy telephone with him. She would talk to him, and then say "your turn," and pause expectantly. He began to mimic her action, pausing to wait for her to take her turn after he said something. This again reinforced the idea of taking turns. When she told the provider what she was doing, the provider began to play similar games with Ahmed.

The provider saw that he was enjoying the game and getting the idea of taking turns rolling the ball, so she invited Angelina into their game. Angelina, a four-and-a-half-year-old, had learned the idea of taking turns pretty well. Soon Angelina and Ahmed were playing the game by themselves.

Let Your Child Have Some Control

As already mentioned, taking turns doesn't come naturally for young children, nor is it easy. So have patience and go slowly. Your child needs many opportunities to have things without sharing them. Give her lots of time with a toy or material she is playing with before asking her to give it up.

Your child may have some toys that she's particularly

attached to and has more difficulty sharing. If another child is coming over to play, ask your child if there are things she doesn't think she can share. Put these things away while the other child is at your house. Your child may not be able to identify these special toys, but if you know she's had trouble giving up a particular toy in the past, you can avoid problems by putting it away before the visitor comes. If your child wants to take a favorite toy to child care (check to be sure your provider allows this), explain to her that she will either have to share it or leave it in her cubby at child care. If this is too difficult for her, tell her that is one toy she cannot take with her.

If another child is over and wants to play with a toy your child is using, let your child control when she wants to let the other child have a turn. You can ask her if she's done or if she wants a few more minutes with it. Allow her to say to the other child, "I want to play alone right now." Respect her need to control the toy awhile longer. Don't lecture or scold. Instead, help the other child find something else to play with. If you must call an end to her turn, ask, "Can Timmy have the dinosaur now or in two minutes?"

You can also let her set some limits on how long or in what way her toys are used by another child. She might be worried that the toy she's lending will not be returned or will be ruined. Help her to say things like "You can look at it, but give it right back," or "You can use it, but don't throw it." Let your provider know that you're using these kinds of phrases so she can use some of the same language. If your child is showing an understanding of these phrases at home, your provider will probably be happy to know that and be able to use something that has proved to be effective.

Begin Coaching

If your preschooler is playing with a friend, take the opportunity to begin coaching her in sharing. If you have more than one child, you probably already have plenty of chances to do this. Help your child learn that when she leaves a toy, another child may use it. This requires being watchful. When you see her getting ready to move to her Lego building blocks, remind her that her brother or her friend will be able to take a turn with the toy she's leaving.

Child care providers may be willing to support your efforts. Large portions of a provider's day are focused on monitoring the children, so she's apt to notice when a child is about to move to another toy. Talk with her about pointing out to your child that a toy becomes open game when she leaves it. This will help to raise her awareness. Given this type of reminder, she might decide to stick with that toy after all, or she may decide she really is done with it.

You and your provider can also coach your child by letting her know when a toy she's been wanting becomes available. If Timmy drops the dinosaur and runs over to pick up a superhero toy, you can say, "Look. Timmy is finished playing with the dinosaur. You can take a turn now."

Praise Success

When your child allows another to play with one of her

toys, notice it out loud. Comment on how much you like it when you see her sharing. If you think your child is in need of special praise, talk with your provider about calling attention to the times when she waits her turn for a snack at child care, or for a turn to use the scissors. Both of you can talk about how good people feel when they share. You can reinforce this by pointing out to your child how good she feels when another child shares with her.

You can also read books to your child that demonstrate sharing and express how good it makes the characters in the book feel. Perhaps you can offer to take the book to child care so the provider also can read it to your child. See if your provider can recommend any good books or sharing games. You can also comment when characters on television or other children in real-life situations are sharing.

Turn-Taking Situations

Take advantage of turn-taking situations that arise normally in the life of your family. For instance, if you take turns passing food at the family dinner table, label this out loud. "Now it's Dad's turn to help himself to some soup." Or label other daily activities. "It's Amy's turn to brush her teeth." You might even arrange some turn-taking opportunities. Let your children take turns choosing which color candles to put on the table or which music to listen to. Take your children, or your child and a friend, to the bakery and take turns ordering a treat.

Child care providers have many opportunities to set

up turn-taking situations for children. They may place chairs at a table to indicate how many children can participate in an activity at one time. They might set up dramatic play areas that encourage sharing, such as a doctor's waiting room, or a deli with numbers for customers to take. They might take the children to the playground and let them take turns on the swings. Talk with your provider about the kinds of turn-taking situations she has available for the children in her care.

You can also warn your child when her turn is almost over, or set a timer that will ring when her turn ends. Most children seem to make plans for their next activity when they hear a warning.

When Someone Has Taken His Toy

If your child comes to you to tell you that someone took the toy he was playing with, he probably wants you to help him get it back. This is an opportunity to teach him some problem-solving skills. If both children have the appropriate verbal skills, you may want to go with him to talk with the other child, but be careful not to barge in with assumptions or blaming. Instead, you can say things like "It looks like both of you want to use the tractor." To help them sort things out, ask a "what" question. For instance, you could ask, "What can you do to work this out?" or "What should you do about that?" or "What can you do that will make you both happy?"

If neither child can come up with a solution, you might say, "One of you can have it first and then it will be the other person's turn." If they can't agree on who should have the first turn, you could do what Ahmed's child care provider sometimes does. She cuts a circle from cardboard and glues red paper to one side and green to the other. She calls her creation a "turn-taker." One child flips the turn-taker; while it's in the air, the other calls out "red" or "green." If it lands on the color called, it's that child's turn first.

You may want to check with your provider to see if your child complains frequently about having things taken from him. If this is the case, pay special attention at home to teaching him problem-solving skills, and ask your provider to give him some extra coaching in this area as well. If he complains frequently that another child has taken a toy after he's left it behind, he may need a reminder that it's okay for another child to use a toy he has left.

When He Takes Someone Else's Toy

Sometimes your child may grab a toy or something a playmate is using. If your child seems to be having trouble with this, spend some extra time supervising closely when he has a playmate over. Again, check with your provider to see if she's observing the same thing. Ask her for help in paying extra attention for a time.

Try to get to your child before he grabs. If you see him hovering and wanting something another child has, you might say, "John is using that. Ask him for a turn. Say, 'John, can I have a turn when you're done?'" Then help him find something else to do while he waits. If the wait is long, help him go back and ask again. He could say, "I've been waiting a really long time. When will you be done?" Teach him to make trades. Help him think of something John may want and then take it to him. Remind him to thank John when he gets his turn.

Be careful to remain calm. If you see your child grab a toy from another child, you may be tempted to teach him a lesson by grabbing that toy away from him. You may think, "I'll show him what it feels like." What you are apt to teach him, however, is that grabbing is okay. He'll see that you grab things and think he can do the same thing. That's the way children's minds work. Instead, stay cool. You might say, "Katie was using that." If he doesn't hand it back, ask him to. If he still doesn't return it, you might say, "You need to give it back. Can you do it by yourself or shall I help you?" If he still doesn't return it, gently return it yourself. Tell him in confidence that other children get angry and don't want to play with him when he grabs their things.

Puppet shows about sharing can be a powerful teaching tool. The story might contain a kernel of a real situation and build on it. Discuss this idea with your provider. She may be interested in doing such a puppet show, or she may welcome your offering to come in and do a puppet show for the children.

If your child seems to be having a lot of trouble with sharing and taking turns, make sure you discuss the situation with your provider. Your child will learn this skill more quickly if the two of you are on the same page. In addition, if your child causes constant disruption at child care because he hasn't learned this skill yet, your provider undoubtedly will appreciate knowing that you're working on the skill at home too. Tell her about specific things you've been doing to encourage your child and about successes you've had.

• • •

Points to Remember and Discuss

- Before the age of three and a half or four, many children are not developmentally ready to share.
- You should allow your child to have some control over his toys or things he's playing with.
- When friends come over, you should put away toys that your child has great difficulty sharing.
- You need to coach your child in asking for a turn. Teach your child assertive phrases to use if the wait becomes too long.
- You can set up situations that allow your child to practice taking turns.
- You should encourage your child to find something to do while he waits for a turn.

Chapter 13
#%*&+!!
Inappropriate Language and Swearing

What's Normal

Perhaps you've felt that flush climb up your face when your precious preschooler shouts out a swear word in front of Grandma, or at a friend's birthday party. "Oh," you think, "now everyone's going to think we use that language at home," you think. Or, "Now everyone will know she heard me say that!"

But even if you're careful never to use "that kind of language," your young child is going to hear it anyway. Children pick up swearing and inappropriate language from other children at the park or at child care, from television, from adults they overhear when they're picking up the car from the mechanic with Dad or at the grocery store with Mom, as well as from their brothers and sisters, and even from their parents.

It's amazing how quickly preschoolers, and even toddlers, pick up the words we don't want them to know.

Perhaps it's because these words are usually delivered with such emotion. Or perhaps they become confused and more curious about such language when we use those words but forbid them from using them. In any event, when children use swear words, they usually get a strong reaction, which makes the words stick in their heads even more.

People have varying tolerance levels for swearing and inappropriate language. Some families are very upset by it; others see it as no big deal. They might look upon swearing as a natural, or at least an acceptable or understandable response on certain occasions. The problem, of course, is that young children have no sense of what an appropriate time or place might be. And if your child swears in the wrong place at the wrong time, it can be very awkward for you and for her.

If foul language is upsetting to parents, it can be at least as upsetting to child care providers. Swearing can spread like flu through a child care center or home. Fortunately, there are ways to teach young children that this type of language is not to be used and to teach them other ways to express themselves.

Don't Overreact

We know that children learn to talk by observation. It seems almost magical: one day they make only nonsensical sounds and the next day "mommy" or "daddy" or "bye" comes tumbling out. Children are paying close attention and are learning language even when we're not aware of it. They learn swear words in the same way. They watch and listen to people.

Adult reactions can make a big difference in whether children continue to use new words they've learned. If adults laugh or get very upset, children may feel powerful. They discover that these words are important. They provoke reactions. They get attention. So try to be matter-of-fact in your response, even if you're taken by surprise.

But don't ignore it. Deal with swearing and foul language the first time you hear it. If you ignore it completely, you may send the message that using foul language is okay. Make it clear that swearing is not acceptable. Say, "That's a word we don't use." Then get your child focused on something else.

Children also come across the words accidentally, by being silly or by experimenting with language. They love rhyming and alliteration, which can lead to all kinds of things. If a swear word pops up accidentally, just help your child continue her fun by playing a rhyming game or reciting a silly poem.

When Other Children Are Using Foul Language

Your child may be hearing swear words on television, from her neighborhood friends, on the playground, or at child care. You can monitor the television your child watches and allow her to watch only shows made for children. You can also pay close attention when she's playing with others, and if you hear another child swearing, you can say to your own child, confidentially, something like "That sounds like something a grown-up might say. It's not okay to say that word." You don't have to speak negatively of the child who swore. Simply make it clear to your child what your expectations are. Let her know that this kind of language can upset other people, and they may not want to be around her if she uses it.

Talk with your child care provider about swearing. Find out if she hears this happening in her setting. She may have a child or two who are experimenting with swearing and she may have been working hard to change the atmosphere. She has the multiple challenge of teaching the child who's using foul language not to swear without shaming him while making it clear to the other children that foul language is not acceptable at child care. She'll appreciate your understanding as well as your support. You can continue to reinforce at home what she is teaching at child care. If your child is in family day care, this is also an opportunity to discuss your provider's policies around having the TV on during the day.

Teaching New Expressions

Sometimes children swear for the same reason adults do: to express frustration or anger. One obvious way to help, then, is to head off frustration. If your child's face is becoming flushed, her voice is getting louder, or she's starting to whine, it's time to help her. Give her ideas about how to handle the frustration, such as asking for help or choosing something different to do.

If your child swears in anger, make it clear that swearing is not acceptable. Then help her learn other words to use in expressing herself. You might say, "I know you're angry. It's okay to say, 'I'm so mad.'" You might also help her expand her feelings vocabulary. Teach her words like "upset" and "frustrated" and "furious" and "annoyed" and "mad" and "cranky." You can also expand her feelings vocabulary beyond words associated with anger. There are common words that have become acceptable substitutes for swear words for most people, words such as "darn," "heck," "shoot," and "son of a gun," that you and your provider may feel comfortable with.

This is something your provider can work on as well. Providers sometimes post charts with faces showing various expressions. Each face is labeled with the word that identifies the feeling being expressed. There are also books that talk about feelings and help children expand their vocabulary. You and your provider can exchange ideas. She may know of books you can pick up from the library or that she can lend to you. You may have books or posters you can share with her.

Attention

Attention is a strong motivator for children, and foul language tends to garner them a lot of attention. You can't always control how much attention your child gets from other children or in other settings when she swears, but you can reduce the attention she gets for swearing at home. You can also influence the attention she gets for swearing in her child care setting by strategizing with your provider. We've already discussed the need to keep your response low-key when your child swears. The other side of the coin is to give your child lots of attention when she behaves appropriately. This is especially true when she is frustrated or angry and uses appropriate language to express herself. You can say, "I'm so glad you're using your words when you're angry. Good for you."

• • •

Points to Remember and Discuss

- You need to deal with swearing the first time you hear it.
- You need to be matter-of-fact. Lots of attention—laughing, scolding, lecturing—may increase a child's interest in swearing.
- You need to make it clear that swearing is not acceptable.
- You can teach your child new words to express her feelings.
- You should reinforce your child when she uses appropriate language.

Chapter 14
I'm Telling on You:
Tattling

What's Normal

Jackson came running to his mother in frustration. He whined, "Sammy hit me, Momma." His mother was busy cooking. She looked down and could see her son wasn't hurt. Her children had been scuffling on and off for the last hour and she was tired of it. She said, "Jackson, stop that tattling. I don't need to have you running in here every two minutes and tattling on your brother."

Jackson's mother's response is understandable and pretty typical of many people. It's tiring to have your children constantly reporting on the negative behavior of another child and waiting for you to fix it. Added to that is the general feeling in our society that we should stay out of other people's business. Tattling is often seen as weak or disloyal, an attitude that can intensify as young children become adolescents and then adults. Hence, our language includes nouns such as "squeal," "snitch," "stool pigeon," or "rat."

Turning away tattling children or ignoring them carries risks in today's society. In our world, children must feel free to report dangers and go to adults for help. Children must feel free to tell a trusted adult when someone is hurting or bothering them or when someone else is in danger. When they are older, children must feel free to tell adults when someone is using drugs or carrying a weapon. There is a difference, of course, between reporting serious problems or danger and a quick resort to whining about every little thing. But if we aren't careful in how we respond, children can get the message that any reporting is weak or wrong.

Parents and child care providers must teach children that telling an adult is the right thing to do in many situations. Adults need to handle the serious situations children face. At the same time, we can teach children how to handle normal, everyday problems on their own. The more problem-solving skills they have, the more independent children will be and the less likely they will be to ask parents and child care providers to intervene.

Listen to What Your Child Has to Say

People sometimes assume a child is telling on another to get the other child in trouble. This may be true, but assumptions can be risky. Don't automatically respond to your child by saying, "She wouldn't do that," or by lecturing on the evils of tattling. Instead, listen to what your child has to say and decide if his complaint is reasonable. If it is, then think about whether he has the skills to handle the problem himself. If you think he does, encourage him to cope with it. If you don't think he has the skills, help him solve the problem. Give him some alternatives to try.

For example, Jackson's mother was with him at the playground when he complained that Ellen wouldn't let him have a turn on the swing. Jackson's mother had coached him in the past on how to ask another child for a turn. So, after listening to his complaint, she asked, "Did you tell Ellen you would like a turn?" Jackson shook his head no, so his mother sent him back to try out his skill.

Later, however, when Jackson came complaining that a bigger boy had shoved him off the slide and hurt his leg, and she could see a bruise just below his knee, she decided to walk over and see what was going on. She discovered a couple of older boys bullying the younger children, so she knew she had to intervene. She told them very clearly that it was not all right to push younger children around and she expected them to share slide time with the young ones. She was very glad she'd listened to Jackson.

From this experience, Jackson got the message that what he had to tell his mother was important, that there were some problems he could solve himself, and that he could get help when he needed it.

It's important that you and your provider share a similar philosophy on this issue. Talk with her to reassure yourself that she respects your feelings about the importance of children being encouraged to tell adults about dangerous or frightening situations. Most child care providers are well aware of creating an atmosphere where children can ask for help. It's part of the curriculum in any early childhood education training. It's also a critical issue that is perfectly fair for you to check out.

If your child seems to be doing a lot of unnecessary reporting, talk with your provider about it. Find out if your child behaves the same way at child care and how she handles it. There are a lot of demands on the attention of child care providers, who sometimes inadvertently overlook a child's need for help in learning how to problem-solve. You might be helping your provider by bringing it to her attention. If, on the other hand, she has noticed and is working with him, you can share information about the kinds of problems your child brings to each of you and whether he's able to use your suggestions for solving problems himself. The two of you can then coordinate your responses.

If both of you find that your child tries the suggestions you give him to solve problems but then comes back for more help, offer to go with him. Your presence will both inspire confidence in him and show your support for him.

Giving Your Child Reassurance

Sometimes children tell on another child because they feel responsible. For instance, you may ask your five-year-old to keep an eye on his two-year-old brother for three minutes while you check the roast in the kitchen. He may feel like he's playing a very important role, and he hears in your request that he's supposed to tell you if his little brother is doing anything wrong. He may transfer this idea to other situations. Later in the day he'll report to you when his little brother throws a toy on the floor. Say, "Thanks for telling me," or "I know," but then clear up his confusion by telling him that, unless you ask, he doesn't need to be in charge.

You can also reassure your child by letting him know that you're aware of what's going on. If, for example, you're at the park and he alerts you that his sister is up high on the jungle gym, you can simply say, "Yes, I'm watching. She's climbing very high, isn't she?" Knowing you're watching may be enough to allow him to return to his play and not worry. If he continues reporting unnecessarily, you can add, "I'll help keep her safe. It's all right for you to play."

Sometimes your child may just be looking for affirmation that he knows and follows the rules. You can simply acknowledge his comment by saying something such as, "I'm glad you know the rules."

And there will no doubt be times when you'll be glad for his report. Perhaps his younger sibling really will be climbing much higher than is safe without your noticing. In such a case, of course, you'll want to thank him for his help.

Making Himself Look Good

There are times when a child will tell on others not because he needs help or because he's worried about them, but because he wants to look good. He wants you to know that he's a "good" child or that his behavior is better than his brother's. He may come to you complaining about his brother calling him a name. If you're pretty sure it's about competition, that he's feeling like his brother gets more attention or is more valued than he is, then acknowledge his comments in a noncommittal way, such as by saying, "Oh" or "I'm sorry you're not getting along." Or you could tell him, "You're very good at figuring out ways to get along with your brother. I'm sure you can tell him you don't like to be called names."

The other part of handling this kind of tattling is building your child's self-esteem during times when he's not telling on others. Comment on his accomplishments and strengths. Let him know often how important he is to you. Give him lots of positive attention.

This is another important juncture for you to talk over with your provider. She also can focus on boosting his self-esteem and giving him extra attention for a while. To get the conversation started, you could say something like Jackson's mom might say: "Jackson has been telling on people a lot lately. I feel like he doesn't know how to take care of some situations on his own. We're trying to offer him ideas at home. How are you handling it at child care?"

Tattling for Power

Tattling can make a child feel powerful, and we all know power feels good. If you overhear your child say, "I'm telling!" he may be using the threat as a way to stop someone from doing something he doesn't want them to do, or in order to get his way. Don't rush in and solve the problem. Hang back and give him a chance to do it on

his own. If he's successful in solving his problem independently, he'll experience a sense of his own internal
competence, and this is much more empowering than
tattling is. If he can't solve his problem on his own, you
can once again offer suggestions and keep on helping
him. When children are just learning to solve conflicts,
they need help thinking of a number of different strategies. You may need to teach him problem-solving skills.
Help him identify the problem, brainstorm solutions,
pick one to try, and evaluate how it worked. Of course,
there are situations in which the lesson to be learned is
how to cope when you don't get your own way.

Children also tattle in order to get someone else in
trouble. If this happens with your child, it probably has
to do with a need for greater attention or self-esteem,
and you can return to the strategies for meeting those
needs. Chapter 6 outlines strategies for giving children
more positive attention.

• • •

Points to Remember and Discuss

- Children need to know that telling an adult is the right
  thing to do in many situations.
- You need to listen to your child before you decide
  whether his tattling is unnecessary.
- Teaching problem-solving skills will reduce the need for
  tattling.
- Children sometimes get mixed messages from adults

about telling on others. Let your child know that she doesn't need to be in charge unless you ask.

- Children may tell on others unnecessarily in order to prove that they're the "good" one, to gain power, or to get others in trouble.

Chapter 15
Let's Say I'm Batman:
Superheroes and Other Play That Includes Aggressive Themes

What's Normal

Many children are drawn to the fast action and exciting themes of superhero play. There are many things to be learned from this kind of dramatic play, including language skills, how to cooperate, how to arrange the parts of a story, and how to negotiate continued play. But these games also have a tendency to become loud and aggressive, and they often have violent themes.

Adults often find pretend aggression and violent themes unsettling. But even pretend aggression has its usefulness. In this type of play, children work on their understanding of good and evil, power and control, right and wrong. They can try on different roles, and conquer imaginary monsters. This kind of play helps children master their fears. The role of parents is to monitor the play closely so it doesn't get out of hand while the children learn and experiment with their notions of good and bad.

Expanding the Play

Children often base their games on television programs or movies. Knowing the characters and plot lines of the programs your child watches can be invaluable. Besides helping you understand your child's play, it also can permit you to make suggestions for building on her play. For instance, if the children have concocted a game based on a show in which one character has recently gone on a camping trip, you can suggest that your child and her playmates go horseback riding or canoeing, as they would in camp.

Your child may be introduced at child care to scenes and characters you don't recognize. She may watch a different program there, or the other children may teach her games from programs they have watched. Your provider can let you know what those programs are so you can educate yourself about them.

You can also help your child expand her play ideas. You can, for instance, help her move away from aggressive play into new adventures by taking her to visit a zoo or a museum or by watching TV shows and movies that encourage cooperation rather than aggression. Children often seek dramatic play with themes that are more exciting than playing house or doctor. You and your child can pack a bag and take an imaginary trip to the land of the dinosaurs, or go on a photo safari. You can explore cardboard box "caves" with a flashlight and magnifying glass, cross a river of hot lava on rope spread on the floor, or build a spaceship to escape the slime monster from Mars. If you have an extra-large box, such as a refrigerator box, you might want to create a cave or a playhouse with it. Or, if your child is in family child care, you can offer the box to your provider, who also might appreciate having props such as extra-large stuffed animals, large posters, or other items that will spur children's imaginations.

You can also help your child expand her play by redirecting superhero activity that is becoming aggressive. You can suggest, for example, that the characters are hungry and want to make a pizza and then help her make a snack (or a pretend pizza out of construction paper or clay). Or you can say the characters are looking for a secret code and then set up a treasure hunt with clues.

Feeling Powerful, Conquering Fear

Preschool children use play that includes aggressive themes to allow themselves to feel powerful. Who is more powerful to a child than Superman or Spider-Man or Wonder Woman? Trying on these roles gives children a chance to act out aggressions in safe ways. It can let them be in charge. You can look for ways your child also can be powerful in your home. She can help to make rules, or decide what to have for supper, or show you her strong muscles as she helps you move chairs to the table.

If your child is working hard on these themes at

home, talk with your provider about giving her appropriate opportunities to feel powerful in the child care setting as well. Perhaps your child can be the one to decide which book to read during reading time this week. One family child care provider begins each day with circle time, and the children take turns being Circle Woman or Circle Man. They call the group to order and announce whose turn it is to undertake different tasks.

Young children also use play that includes aggressive themes to help them conquer their fears. Children wrestle with all kinds of monsters—monsters in their closets, under their beds, in the media, from their nightmares, in their heads, sometimes even the real-life monsters of angry or threatening adults. It helps them master their fears if they can set up and control the action in the light of day. Although a monster may be invading from outer space or coming up from the deep, your child magically has the power to banish it. If your child is doing things like this, you can help her get rid of the monsters by ordering them out of here "Right now!"

If your child is having difficulty recognizing the line between what is real and what is pretend, help her identify her feelings by asking a question such as "Some pretend things seem very real, don't they?" Talk with her about how actors are so good at pretending, that it looks real. You might act out a favorite story, perhaps "The Three Billy Goats Gruff," and let her be the actor. You might want to ask your provider if your child seems to be working on conquering fears at child care as well. Describe to her the kinds of play your child has been designing at home. And, of course, let her know if there are specific fears your child is dealing with in real life so your provider can be alert to helping your child deal with those fears.

Here is one example of how coordination between parent and provider can be used to make superhero play even more useful to a child. Mary's neighbor's house had been broken into recently and Mary was having nightmares about monsters breaking into her bedroom at night. Her parents talked with her about what had happened, reassured her they would keep her safe, and showed her that the doors were locked at night. Her father also told the child care provider what had happened, so when Mary got frantic about checking a closet door at child care, the provider wasn't puzzled. The provider then suggested a game in which the inhabitants of a castle banish all the monsters from their home.

Keeping the Play Creative

Some of the toys marketed for superhero play are made to suggest they can be used in only one way. Advertising can make a child believe that she needs more toys if she wants to do something different. For example, a manufacturer might want your child to believe that one doll is for giving baths and another doll is for exercising. You can help your child understand that the same doll can be used for virtually anything she can imagine. You can also choose toys that allow your child to use them in any number of ways, such as Lego building blocks or playdough. And you can help your child create her own props.

What About Weapons?

Many people don't want their children to play with toy guns or swords or other toy weapons. Yet children seem to have a strong urge to play with such things. No matter what you say, children will find a way to pretend they have guns or swords. It seems to be part of learning to master their aggression.

Still, you can redirect your child by showing him other kinds of props, or you can encourage him to create his own gizmos for tracking danger. Can he make a radar detector, a walkie-talkie, or a laser device that makes people invisible? Perhaps he and his playmates will want to protect the town from a natural disaster such as a forest fire or a hurricane, or from a tiger that has escaped from the zoo. Making suggestions like these takes the focus off fighting other people and onto a cooperative effort. You can also restrict the amount of superhero programming or video games with violent themes your child is exposed to at home and make the same request to your home child care provider.

Some providers allow toy guns in the home or center. Others may not. If you have strong feelings about not allowing your child to play with toy guns, talk with your provider about it. Whatever you and your provider decide about allowing toy weapons, remember that your child needs to play games with exciting themes. Work together on suggestions for dramatic play with exciting themes that do not involve weapons. You might say, "I share your concern that the children not learn to be aggressive. I don't want that either. But I know my daughter loves adventure. Do the children here ever play games like going on a photo safari or investigating caves?"

Turning from Play to Real Aggression

Active, dramatic play can get so exciting or so chaotic that your child will need help containing it. Watch for signs that play is getting aggressive: louder, higher-pitched voices, more arguments about who will do what, trouble sharing props. If you sense this happening, join your child and his playmates and help them resolve the conflict. Help them identify the problem and think about ways it can be worked out. You can also use their play to teach them about peacemaking. You might say something like "Can the Power Rangers find another way to work things out besides fighting?"

Sometimes you'll need to help your child and her playmates draw their play to a close. A good way to do that is to create a logical ending for their story. Here's an example that one parent came up with. "After a big pizza supper, the Teenage Mutant Ninja Turtle is very sleepy. Put him to bed for a while and choose something quiet to do." You can then guide your child and her playmates to another, quieter activity such as using playdough or coloring or reading books.

Your provider may enlist your help in curbing super-hero play. It can be more difficult to control this type of play at a child care setting with many children than it is at home. Your provider may ask parents about the programs their children watch and suggest that they cut back on programming with violent themes. Try to be open to such suggestions from your provider. It may not seem like much to you, but it can have a big impact in settings where many children in close quarters can get really wound up. It can be difficult to control a child's exposure to media violence, but violent programming does have a strong effect on children. It is well worth doing what you can to carefully choose the programming your preschooler routinely watches.

• • •

Points to Remember and Discuss

- Children use superhero play and other play with aggressive themes to help them feel powerful and to help them conquer fears.
- You can help your child find creative props to expand such play.
- You can offer your child suggestions for expanding or redirecting such play.
- You need to watch for signs that play is becoming too aggressive—loud voices or arguments, for example—and guide your child to calmer, quieter activities.
- You should monitor and restrict your child's access to TV programming and movies with violent themes.

Chapter 16
Whack! Chomp! Ouch!
Aggressive Behavior

What's Normal

You may feel bad the first time you see your child hit someone or throw a toy in apparent anger. You may wonder if you've done something wrong, or if there's something wrong with your child. Although there is disagreement about exactly how people come to be aggressive, one thing is clear: aggression is a normal part of human development.

"Many children discover the use of physical aggression before" they are a year old. One large study in Canada involving 20,000 children "found that the use of physical aggression peaks between the ages of twenty-seven and twenty-nine months." Beginning when children are about two-and-a-half, physically aggressive behavior slowly begins to decrease. By the time they reach kindergarten, most children are relatively peaceful (Barbara Kaiser and Judy Sklar Rasminsky, *Challenging Behavior in Young Children*).

While some aggressive behavior is normal, it's also something that demands prompt attention, because children learn to be peaceful beings only when they are taught to be so. A number of studies have shown that cultures that encourage aggressive behavior are aggressive societies, and cultures that discourage it are peaceful societies. Families and child care providers must teach children how to get their needs met in direct, respectful, and peaceful ways.

Aggression takes various forms. It may be direct, like hitting or pushing, and designed to help a child get what he or she wants. Or it may be a reaction to feeling frustrated, angry, or out of control. Also, as we say in Chapter 15, children may use aggression in their play.

Sudden bouts of aggression also can be a sign of frustration over something new at home or child care that's upsetting your child. Such bouts will subside if you can identify the issue and deal with it. But if your child seems to be more aggressive than other children both at home and at child care on an ongoing basis and there's no improvement despite all you and your provider do, you might seek professional help to determine whether a medical or psychological reason underlies this behavior.

Accidental Aggression

Sometimes children are aggressive unintentionally. For instance, Kayla would often initiate play by bumping her shoulder into another child. Although her parents didn't notice this at home very much, it showed up at child care, where there were lots of children to interact with and where getting attention was not always easy.

When the child care provider saw this, she would walk over to Kayla, bend down beside her, and gently say, "Kayla, why don't you pat Jeremy's back lightly to get his attention?" She found herself doing this repeatedly for a couple of weeks. She also concentrated on noticing when Kayla reached out to playmates in a nonthreatening way. The first time she saw Kayla patting Jeremy's back, she praised her. "You did a great job of getting Jeremy's attention, Kayla."

Aggression can be an accidental part of trying to be social, so teaching your child appropriate social skills can quickly stem the aggression. Because child care providers constantly work with groups of children, they're apt to deal with this kind of aggression more frequently than you do at home. Your provider may be able to give you ideas for teaching your child how to get attention from other children in a socially acceptable way. For ideas to help your child join in the play of others, look back at Chapter 11.

Another type of accidental aggression occurs when children just can't keep their hands to themselves. If you've ever taken a family car trip with more than one child in the backseat, you'll recognize this phenomenon. Children have a lot of trouble sitting still. They wriggle and squirm and explore, and in the process they bump and touch and bang into each other. Again, since your child care provider frequently manages multiple children in close quarters, she may have good ideas about how to handle this. Providers often mark off individual spaces with tape on the floor or with carpet squares, or they use assigned seats. You can try some of these same techniques at home. For instance, if you have more than one child, give each child his or her own special place at the dinner table. You can also have your child pretend there's a bubble around his personal space and practice staying inside that bubble.

Misinterpreting an Accident

Accidents can lead to aggression. For example, your child accidentally knocks over the block tower her older brother has carefully constructed. Her brother sees this, gets mad, and shoves his little sister. You can help by quickly describing the situation as accidental. "Sonya accidentally knocked down your blocks when she tried to get to her building." To head off this kind of physically aggressive behavior, make sure each child has plenty of space for playing.

You may also need to intervene when your child has playmates over. For instance, if two children are sitting on the couch watching television, your son may decide he wants to sit with them and try to climb in between them. You may need to be quick in saying, "Doug accidentally pushed you over because he wants to sit by you."

Roughhousing also can foster accidents that turn into aggression. Many children love to wrestle, roll around, and tumble over each other. To prevent such play from becoming hurtful, you need to provide plenty of space and appropriate equipment for it. For instance, you might want to limit rough play to outdoors, or to a large playroom with a carpet on the floor. And be sure the children understand that there's to be no hitting, pinching, or biting and that they must stop if one of them says, "Stop."

Children often need help calming down after high-energy play. Just saying "Play something else now" may not be enough; you may need to guide them in moving to another, calmer activity. Sensory activities are effective in helping children calm themselves. Try giving them, for instance, some clay or sand or perhaps some fingerpainting materials, all of which are soothing to play with.

Child care centers often can provide an opportunity for children to indulge in rough-and-tumble play. Centers may have areas with large motor equipment or open areas with mats or mattresses where young children can safely engage in very physical play. Although family child care is not as apt to be set up with such areas, a family child care provider can take children to the park or the local YMCA or to other locations where they can play actively. You may want to accompany your provider on some of these trips, to watch how your child does, to learn techniques for preventing aggression, and to help monitor the group to ensure that aggression doesn't result from high-energy activities.

Hitting, Kicking, Screaming, Pushing, Shoving

Sometimes your child will use aggressive behavior intentionally to get what she wants or simply because she's so frustrated or angry that she can't control herself. It's essential that you stem this kind of behavior. Make it very clear that aggression is not permitted. You might say to your child, "I won't let you hit your brother. Hitting hurts."

Never hit your child in order to teach him not to hit. What you'll teach him instead is that bigger, more powerful people can control less powerful people with aggression. Of course, your provider should never hit or threaten to hit your child either. It is rare to find a provider who would hit or spank a child. For a licensed provider, this kind of behavior could threaten her license. It's important that you know your provider's practices and feelings concerning corporal punishment.

If your child does a lot of hitting, consult with your provider. Make sure both of you are quick to intervene and set limits. Work together on teaching him to use his words instead of his hands or feet. Suggest words he can use, such as "Stop," "That's mine," or "Help." If your child's language skills are well enough developed, he can use more complex sentences, such as "I was using that," or "When can I have a turn?" When he does use his words in a situation of conflict, praise him. Ask your provider to do the same.

If your child has a volatile temperament and gets out of control quickly, it's especially important to work closely with your provider. You can work together on teaching your child to recognize when she is angry and to calm herself. Help her stop and think about what she should do when she's angry. Coach her to say to herself, "Don't hit." Teach her to take deep breaths to help her relax. You can make a game out of taking belly breaths by having her lie on the floor and watch her belly rise and fall as she takes deep breaths. This will help her become used to the sensation and to realize what you're talking about when she's angry and you coach her to breathe deeply. You can also play the stop-and-freeze game described in Chapter 5. Ask your provider if she could take the time to play these games at child care.

If your child finds it impossible to stop hitting, she may need to choose a different, quiet activity to do by herself for a while. You might want to direct her to a quiet spot with a book or have her listen to music with headphones. Find out what kinds of activities your provider diverts her toward when she can't seem to stop hitting. Once she's in control of her emotions, she can rejoin you or the other child or children she was playing with.

Be aware, too, of what is being modeled for your child. Seeing a lot of fighting at home, in her neighborhood, or on television will influence her. If she's watching a lot of violent programming, eliminate it and, if your child is in a home setting, be sure your provider will do the same.

To monitor your child's use of aggression in her child care setting, stay in close touch with your provider. Perhaps, until your child's aggressive behavior diminishes, a weekly check-in would be useful. Ask your provider to give you examples of times when she's been able to help your child solve a problem peacefully. This will give you a chance to build on what she's doing, and it will let you acknowledge your provider's good work and show her your appreciation, always important aspects of building a good relationship.

Help with Problem Solving

Learning problem-solving skills will lessen the need your child feels to behave aggressively. This technique is especially useful with older preschoolers. A four-and-a-half- or five-year-old child really can begin to learn conflict resolution skills.

Help the children involved to identify the problem, brainstorm to come up with possible solutions, pick one to try, and then evaluate how it worked. Problem-solving meetings can help everyone calm down. First ask each child what happened. Then start problem solving by asking, "What can you do that will make both of you happy?" If they're unable to come up with any solutions, suggest a few.

Biting

Biting is a form of aggressive behavior that is in a category all by itself, not because it's a more egregious type of aggression, but because adults often find it to be the most unsettling. It's generally more common among children between the ages of fourteen and twenty-four months and among young preschool children who aren't yet very verbal. Children may bite when they are frustrated, overstimulated, angry, or hungry. They also may bite to soothe the pain of teething.

Biting is very upsetting for the child who bites, for the child who is bitten, and for parents or providers. When biting breaks the skin, medical attention may be required. Keep in mind, however, that it is not a catastrophe. What's most important is that you remain calm.

Take a few deep breaths, help the children calm down, and then deal with what has happened.

As with other kinds of misbehavior, biting often occurs when children are tired, hungry, or frustrated. They are much more apt to fall apart under stressful circumstances. So tailor your schedule to make sure your child gets rest and food at the times he needs them, and watch to make sure your child is not becoming too frustrated or stimulated by an activity. If his face is becoming flushed, his voice is growing louder, or his breathing is becoming more rapid, you may need to intervene immediately, before he reaches the point of biting.

As with other types of aggressive behavior, you can help your child avoid biting by teaching him to use his words and removing him to another quiet activity if he cannot calm himself.

Your child may be biting because he is jealous of a younger brother or sister, or because an older brother or sister takes his toys away. If your child is having trouble with biting, you may need to make sure that either he or his sibling is with you at all times in order to protect them both. If your child is biting you, be clear that this is not okay. If you are holding him, put him down and say, "Biting hurts. I don't like it when you bite me." Withhold your attention for a short time and then return to dealing with your child.

Make sure you tell your provider if your child is having trouble with biting. She can then coordinate her responses with yours so you're both giving your child the same message. She also needs to know in order to protect the other children in her care. On the other hand, you may hear from your provider that your child is biting, even though you've never seen this behavior at home. Your child may be less apt to bite when he's with you than when he's in child care. This is especially true if in his child care setting he is with a number of other young children. If this is the case, your provider will appreciate your efforts at attending to your child's needs for rest and food so he doesn't arrive at child care at the edge of his coping ability.

You may want to discuss intervention strategies with your provider and ask her to track the number of biting incidents. This will help you get a handle on the severity of your child's problems. It will also help you recognize growth and improvement as his coping skills improve and the number of incidents decreases.

• • •

Points to Remember and Discuss

- Aggressive behavior is a normal part of human development.
- Children can be taught to inhibit their aggression—or to be more aggressive.
- Children may be aggressive by accident, or to get what they want, or because their emotions are out of control.
- A child with aggressive behavior who doesn't respond to interventions over time may need the attention of a health care professional.

- You need to make it clear to your child that aggressive behavior is not permitted.
- You can teach your child other ways to express himself or reach his goals.
- You cannot teach children to stop hitting or biting by hitting or biting them.

Chapter 17
Philosophies on Childrearing

Throughout this book, we've referred to developmental information and good childrearing practices. This final chapter summarizes the latest information about childrearing practices that nurture self-esteem, confidence, good social skills, and a caring attitude.

Teaching, Not Blaming

Beginning in Chapter 1, we've emphasized that experience and research show that the best way to help your child learn new behaviors is through guidance rather than punishment. Teaching works better than blaming. Here are some basic principles of a guidance approach to raising children.

>Build a Loving Relationship

Your relationship with your child is the foundation on which all teaching and learning is based. Paying positive attention to your child, letting him know you love him no matter what, is the most important thing you can do. It is the beginning of all learning.

Most parents already know how to pay positive attention. It begins with responding to your child's basic
needs for food and warmth and cleanliness. You spend
time with your child, pay attention to what she likes and
doesn't like, play with her, follow her lead when you play
together, cuddle her, tell her you love her, soothe her
when she's hurt or frightened, take a break when your
frustration or anger feels overwhelming.

You don't have to be perfect, of course. All parents
make mistakes, get inappropriately angry sometimes, and
don't always notice when their child needs them. You
only have to be good enough. Just know that your child,
underneath it all, is not trying to be "bad." She's learning
how to express her needs and, most of all, she wants to
please you.

> Show Your Child Acceptance

Your attitude makes all the difference when you want to
get your child to change his behavior. You're apt to handle a situation very differently if you think that your
child is out to get you rather than that he is confused, or
doesn't realize he isn't supposed to behave a certain way,
or is simply motivated by fun and curiosity. For example,
when Ben was helping his mother bake, he put his hands
into the bowl of flour and scattered some of it as he
pulled his hands out. His mother could have assumed
Ben was being sloppy and didn't care about keeping
things clean. Or she could have assumed he was having
so much fun he didn't realize that flour was flying.

Depending upon her attitude, Ben's mother could
choose very different ways to handle this situation. Tone

of voice, facial expressions, and body language reflect a parent's feelings. They also speak louder than words. If you believe your child is misbehaving on purpose, you're more likely to frown and use a demanding voice to tell him, "You need to clean up this mess. Come on, get busy. Come! Now!" Your child, then, would be likely to hear negative messages about himself and feel anxious.

Fortunately, although his mother knew Ben needed to learn to clean up his messes, she didn't see what he'd done as naughty behavior. She was able to remain matter-of-fact, and she encouraged him by saying, "When you were playing with the flour, some of it fell out. I need you to clean up your spills. Here's the whisk broom and the dustpan. I'll use the broom and help." She assumed Ben wasn't aware of the mess or didn't see it as a problem and that he needed more information or direction to clean up. When you use a guidance approach, you teach your child that he's responsible and that he can do many things for himself.

> Don't Rush to Conclusions

If your child is misbehaving, take time to watch closely and figure out what's really going on. This will help you decide what kind of help your child needs in order to change her behavior. For instance, if you notice that your child has started throwing toys, pay close attention to when that happens. Maybe it happens when she's really tired or hungry. Notice what's going on just before it happens and just after it happens. Maybe your child is responding to frustration. Maybe she throws a toy when she can't get it to do what she wants it to do. Or maybe it happens when another child does something that upsets her. Whatever it is, you'll be better able to teach her not to throw toys if you understand why she's doing it and help her gain the skills to respond differently. If she starts throwing toys just before naptime, you may need to get her to her bed earlier. If she throws her doll when she can't get the doll's jacket over its arm, you may need to sit down and show her how to put the jacket on. You might coach your child to come and ask you for help when she's having trouble. You'll probably need to closely observe what happens several times before you get a good idea of what's prompting your child's behavior. It also can be helpful to observe other children her age.

>Make Child-Friendly Space in Your House

The physical environment in your home can help your child learn independence and self-control, two skills that are crucial in the preschool years. Parents disagree about "baby proofing" their homes. Some parents believe a child should be able to learn "no" and simply obey. Toddlers, however, are only just beginning to learn self-control. It may be asking too much of a toddler to leave a precious glass figurine that belonged to your grand-mother at his eye level. This is true for preschoolers as well. You're taking a chance if you leave precious, break-able things within your young child's reach. It's especially important never to leave dangerous items such as sharp knives or matches within a child's reach. Children need a safe space where they can move freely as they explore and learn.

Children also need to be able to make choices and do

things for themselves. If your child constantly pulls at your shirt, saying "Play with me," it's possible she needs more play opportunities within her reach. This can promote independence. Most parents can't set up their home like a child care center, with a playhouse area, a building area, and so on. But there are things you can do to make it easier for your child to help herself when playing. For instance, if your child loves to color and cut and make things, you might designate a special drawer for her that is stocked with a child's scissors, construction paper, glue, and crayons. Store your child's toys on low shelves rather than in a toy box, where toys often get lost or broken.

Lots of times changing a space is the answer to a behavior problem. For instance, if your child never puts her coat on a hanger, you might install a hook in the closet that's easy for her to use. Or look at what the child care center uses and set up something similar at home. Maybe you need to keep fewer toys out at one time so your child isn't overwhelmed when it's time to clean up. If the blocks never get put back into their original box, you might substitute a plastic container that's easier to use than the original box.

>Keep a Regular Schedule

Children do better with regular schedules. Think about it: Even for us adults, life feels safer when it's reasonably predictable. It's even more important for young children who are just learning their way in the world. It's comforting to them to know what to expect from their days. If your child still naps, try to make it the same time every day. If he gets a snack when he awakens, offer one consistently. Keep in mind, too, that it helps a child pace himself if you alternate high-energy activities with quiet ones.

You may even be able to make your days at home somewhat consistent with your child's schedule at child care. Perhaps you can do your outings in the morning if that's when your provider does hers. Try to keep nap routines similar. If naptime is still observed at child care, although your child doesn't nap anymore, you might ask your child to spend some quiet time alone with books during the period when naptime normally would occur. This may make it easier for your child to cooperate with the schedule in child care. This isn't always practical, of course, and you can't be rigid about it. It may make more sense for you to do an outing in the afternoon, or your child may be too excited by a visit from Grandma to observe quiet time some afternoons. Still, to the extent that you can keep your home schedule regular and somewhat similar to that at child care, it can be helpful.

It will also help both you and your child if you give him a bit of advance warning when you're going to do something different. Let him know ahead of time, for example, that you plan to go to the store when lunch is finished. Make it very clear what he needs to do when that time comes. You might say, "Put your coat on and wait for me by the front door," or, "In ten minutes we're going to have lunch." Then, when it's time for lunch, you can say, "We're going to eat now. Will you please put all the blocks into their container and come into the kitchen?" Plenty of warning and very clear instructions make transitions easier for children.

>Match Age to Activities and Toys

Make sure the activities you do with your child or those you expect your child to do alone are appropriate for her age. If you find your child acting out, perhaps she's frustrated because a toy or activity is too difficult for her. Four-year-olds can get very frustrated trying to dress Barbie dolls. And three-year-olds, although they can use large interlocking blocks, may not have the fine motor coordination required to manipulate Lego building blocks.

>Teach New Behavior to Replace Old Behavior

A classic example of teaching new behavior is saying the phrase "Use your words instead of your fists." You obviously want to teach your child that hitting his playmates is not all right, but it may not be enough to just say, "Don't hit Johnny. That hurts him." Your child needs to learn the skills to handle the situation the next time it comes up. If he's upset with Johnny, he needs to know what behavior will work. So, after you tell him not to hit, you might say, "Use your words. Tell Johnny you don't want him to knock over your blocks." Similarly, if your child is swearing, it may not be enough to say, "Stop swearing." You could add, "There are better words you can use. You can say, 'That hurt me,' or 'I'm mad.'"

In Summary

Researchers constantly increase their knowledge about the developmental stages all children go through. Based on that information, we've tried in this book to offer some guidelines for understanding and meeting behavioral challenges both at home and as a partner with your provider at child care. These guidelines can be applied to many different styles of parenting. What's important is that you and your provider work together to understand your child's behavior and find mutually satisfying and effective ways to nurture the natural growth and blossoming of your unique child.

• • •

Points to Remember and Discuss

- As children develop and learn, they behave in ways that may feel challenging to adults.
- Challenging behavior is normal for children.
- Your child's learning is built on the foundation of a loving relationship.
- It takes time and close attention to understand why a child is acting in a certain way.
- Your child needs safe, comfortable spaces.
- Your child needs a regular schedule, nutritious food, and enough rest.
- Your child needs age-appropriate toys.
- Your child needs to be taught what to do as well as what not to do.

Choosing Quality Child Care

Because profound growth and change occur during the first five years of a child's life, the child care experience you choose can play a significant role in your child's physical, social, emotional, and cognitive development. The child care field has responded to increased awareness of the importance of early learning and development by offering families a variety of quality care options.

Setting Goals That Meet Your Childs Needs

As you go about choosing child care, keep in mind the goals and values that are uniquely important to your family. Remember that what may be an ideal care arrangement for a neighbor or a coworker may not be what works well for your child or family. If it's important to you that siblings who need care have plenty of time together, you'll probably want to look for a licensed home or a center where children are in mixed-age groups. If, on the other hand, you believe your child would benefit from a larger group experience with the opportunity to interact with a variety of children and adults, you might want to look at child care centers.

Just as there are many different parenting styles, quality child care comes in many different models. It's important that you choose a model and setting that both supports your family values and goals and meets the quality standards you decide are essential for your child. Rates vary by type of program, qualifications of staff, adult-child ratios, and demographics, and better programs often cost more. If a program you like is priced outside your budget, look into funding assistance options such as the child care tax credit and dependent-care flex spending accounts.

Before choosing a child care setting, take the time to carefully consider your answers to these questions:

- What is my child like? What personality traits have emerged?
- What are my child's special needs now? What possible future needs might my child have?
- What are my child's interests? Have any special skills become apparent?
- What are my family's practical needs—schedule, budget, and so on?
- What values and traditions—religious and cultural ones, for instance—are important to my family?
- What goals do I have for my child? Do I want my child to:

    >learn how to play well with others?

    >be more independent and confident?

>be prepared for school?
>have a fun, safe experience?

Child Care Options

Although there are a variety of child care models—some based on a specific philosophy or approach, such as Montessori or Reggio, and others with a religious or cultural focus—there are three basic settings in which child care is delivered.

- In-Home Care. The caregiver, who may be a family member, a friend, or a professional provider, comes into your home.
- Family Child Care. The caregiver provides care for your child and other children, usually of various ages, in his or her home. Family child care providers should be licensed or registered by your state or county agency.
- School-Based or Independent Child Care Centers. Your child is cared for by a staff—usually one trained in early childhood education—in a regulated setting that often has educationally designed play areas and a schedule of programmed activities for children grouped by age.

To find out about programs available in your area, look up your regional Child Care Resource and Referral Agency. Because they vary from state to state, you'll need to ask your local agency what the licensing requirements and standards are for your state. You can also ask your agency if any violations have been reported for centers or homes on your list of prospective settings.

Visiting Child Care Settings

Selecting the type of child care that will work best for your family may take some time. It's important that you visit each child care setting you're considering (seeing a minimum of three is recommended) and, if possible, that you revisit the settings you liked the first time around. While visiting, pay attention to the interactions of the children with each other and with the provider. For a significant portion of any given day, the atmosphere should be pleasant, the children should be engaged in stimulating activities, and the provider should be interacting with or available to the children.

When children are involved, conflicts are inevitable. If a conflict arises while you're visiting, you'll have a wonderful opportunity to see whether the provider responds in a caring and developmentally appropriate way and is sensitive to the children's emotional needs. As they grow and develop, children experience anger and sadness along with all the joys and happiness of childhood. They need the support of knowledgeable, caring adults as they learn to identify and deal with their emotions effectively. In quality child care settings, children receive a lot of adult attention and assistance in learning how to identify and manage their emotions as they participate in activities and interact with other children and adults.

As part of each visit, you'll want to ask the provider or director about her setting's policies and practices.

Common policy issues and topics to ask about include injuries and illness, emergencies and disasters, being late, holidays and vacations, bringing toys and other personal belongings from home, television watching, behavior challenges and discipline, toilet training, parent communication and conferences, safety and security, and meals and nutrition. Most homes and centers should have written-down policies. Ask for a copy. If topics you need to know about aren't covered, ask the provider about them and add that information to your copy for future reference.

Quality Child Care Environments

Each child care setting you visit will be different, and the facilities of child care centers will be very different from home care settings. But in any setting, there are general benchmarks of quality care to look for. During a reasonable length of time in a child care setting, you should see these indicators of quality:

1. Children are given the opportunity to engage in large-motor activities, including
- building, sorting, and stacking with a variety of materials such as large blocks;
- organized active small group games and exercises;
- free time to run, jump, and climb both outside and in, in groups and individually.

2. Social interaction is facilitated both formally in small group activities and informally in play with another child or with several other children.

3. Children are given opportunities to develop emerging literacy, math, science, and artistic skills through age-appropriate play and manipulation of materials of a variety of sizes, shapes, and colors:

- interesting objects to count and sort
- blocks and puzzles for learning spatial relationships
- markers, crayons, and pencils for writing and drawing
- books to read and to have read to them
- building materials that promote problem solving and emerging math skills
- games that involve matching, sequencing, and classification, which are the cornerstones for math and reading

4. Children's creativity is encouraged through opportunities to engage in painting, drawing, singing, dancing, storytelling, and playing with puppets, dolls, and toy animals.

5. The environment is clean and safe for all the children because

- children are supervised at all times by an adult (a minimum adult-to-child ratio of one to four for infants and one to ten for preschool ages is recommended);
- the toys are appropriate for the age of the children and are in good condition;
- there are no safety hazards such as stairs without proper railings, exposed wiring, uncovered outlets, access to tools or medicine, or dangerous pets;

- infants and toddlers are protected from the rough play of older children;
- the atmosphere is pleasant and inviting to children and their families;
- the setting is usually calm and often is filled with the happy sounds of children playing;
- the provider speaks to the children respectfully and maintains discipline without shouting or threatening;
- the children have a secure place where they can keep their personal belongings.

Accreditation

Accreditation is the status given to early childhood programs that have completed an extensive evaluation process based on state and national standards for quality care. To become accredited, a program must participate in an extensive self-study that includes parent evaluation and observation by a trained validation expert. Both child care centers and family child programs may be accredited. Accreditation, however, is not a guarantee of quality. It is a voluntary system to set professional standards and to help families identify high-quality programs. It is simply one tool for helping families evaluate and choose child care.

Provider Credentials

The most important component of quality child care is the relationship your child has with the care provider. Children who have nurturing, responsive, and stable relationships with caring adults generally grow up to be healthier and more competent than children who don't. Research has shown that relationships are a key component to healthy brain development. While observing a child care setting, be sure to look for indications of the relationships the provider has with individual children as well as her rapport with the group. Some questions you may want to ask the provider include the following:

- What experience do you have in working with children, especially children who have characteristics similar to my child's?

- What is your educational experience? The educational requirements for child care providers vary from state to state. Provider credentials can include the completion of a few specific courses, a two-year or four-year college degree in early childhood development, a child development associate degree, a teaching degree, or even a master's degree. Regardless of the type of education a provider has, she or he should be licensed or certified. Studies have shown that one of the best predictors of quality child care is the amount of ongoing training and education the provider receives.

- [if the child care setting is a center] Who are all the people who would be caring for my child and what are their qualifications?

- How long might my child be with a particular provider or teacher? [In other words, what are the teacher turnover rates and, if the children transition to other providers or teachers as they age, how is that transition conducted?]

- What is your philosophy on the care and education of children and what methods do you use? [In other words, how well does the provider's viewpoint fit your family's values and goals?]

The Parent/Provider Relationship

As stressed in this and the other books in this series, the best child care arrangement is one in which the parents and provider work together to provide the guidance, nurturing, and experiences that foster the child's growth and development. A professional child care provider recognizes the parent as the most important influence on the child's development. Good parenting includes seeking information about your child's behavior, interests, skills, and development from knowledgeable resources such as a professional provider. The best way to ensure quality child care is to maintain daily, meaningful communication with your chosen child care provider and to become actively involved in parent activities. Whether you choose a family child care, a child care center, or a professional to care for your child in your home, a quality child care experience should promote your child's health, growth, and education in a fun and safe setting.

Resources for Finding Quality Child Care
www.childcareaware.org (800-424-2246)
A national organization to assist families with child care. This site includes a tool to search for family and center child care in your area. Offered in both English and Spanish.

www.naeyc.org
The National Association for the Education of Young

Children. This site has information on accreditation for families as well as a search function for accredited child care centers and kindergartens in your area.

www.nafcc.org
The National Association for Family Child Care. This site has a search function for accredited family child care in your area.

About the Author

Deborah Hewitt is an early childhood teacher, consultant, and author of *So This Is Normal Too? Teachers and Parents Working Out Developmental Issues in Young Children*. She lives in Brooklyn Park, Minnesota.

For over thirty years, Redleaf Press has been a leading publisher of exceptional professional resources for the early childhood field. Redleaf Guides for Parents offer parents field-tested, cutting-edge thinking about creating positive partnerships with the adults who care for their children.